MznLnx

Missing Links Exam Preps

Exam Prep for

Beginning Algebra

Miller & O'Neill, 1st Edition

The MznLnx Exam Prep is your link from the texbook and lecture to your exams.
The MznLnx Exam Preps are unauthorized and comprehensive reviews of your textbooks.

All material provided by MznLnx and Rico Publications (c) 2010
Textbook publishers and textbook authors do not particpate in or contribute to these reviews.

MznLnx

Rico
Publications

Exam Prep for Beginning Algebra
1st Edition
Miller & O'Neill

Publisher: Raymond Houge	*Product Manager:* Dave Mason
Assistant Editor: Michael Rouger	*Editorial Assitant:* Rachel Guzmanji
Text and Cover Designer: Lisa Buckner	*Pedagogy:* Debra Long
Marketing Manager: Sara Swagger	*Cover Image:* Jim Reed/Getty Images
Project Manager, Editorial Production: Jerry Emerson	*Text and Cover Printer:* City Printing, Inc.
Art Director: Vernon Lowerui	*Compositor:* Media Mix, Inc.

(c) 2010 Rico Publications
ALL RIGHTS RESERVED. No part of this work covered by the copyright may be reproduced or used in any form or by an means--graphic, electronic, or mechanical, including photocopying, recording, taping, Web distribution, information storage, and retrieval systems, or in any other manner--without the written permission of the publisher.

For more information about our products, contact us at:
Dave.Mason@RicoPublications.com

For permission to use material from this text or product, submit a request online to:
Dave.Mason@RicoPublications.com

Printed in the United States
ISBN:

Contents

CHAPTER 1
REFERENCE: FRACTIONS, DECIMALS, PERCENTS, GEOMETRY, AND STUDY SKILLS — 1

CHAPTER 2
SET OF REAL NUMBERS — 13

CHAPTER 3
LINEAR EQUATIONS AND INEQUALITIES — 25

CHAPTER 4
POLYNOMIALS AND PROPERTIES OF EXPONENTS — 40

CHAPTER 5
FACTORING POLYNOMIALS — 54

CHAPTER 6
RATIONAL EXPRESSIONS — 65

CHAPTER 7
GRAPHING LINEAR EQUATIONS IN TWO VARIABLES — 75

CHAPTER 8
SYSTEMS OF LINEAR EQUATIONS IN TWO VARIABLES — 85

CHAPTER 9
RADICALS — 93

CHAPTER 10
FUNCTIONS, COMPLEX NUMBERS, AND QUADRATIC EQUATIONS — 104

ANSWER KEY — 110

TO THE STUDENT

COMPREHENSIVE

The *MznLnx* Exam Prep series is designed to help you pass your exams. Editors at MznLnx review your textbooks and then prepare these practice exams to help you master the textbook material. Unlike study guides, workbooks, and practice tests provided by the texbook publisher and textbook authors, *MznLnx* gives you **all** of the material in each chapter in exam form, not just samples, so you can be sure to nail your exam.

MECHANICAL

The MznLnx Exam Prep series creates exams that will help you learn the subject matter as well as test you on your understanding. Each question is designed to help you master the concept. Just working through the exams, you gain an understanding of the subject--its a simple mechanical process that produces success.

INTEGRATED STUDY GUIDE AND REVIEW

MznLnx is not just a set of exams designed to test you, its also a comprehensive review of the subject content. Each exam question is also a review of the concept, making sure that you will get the answer correct without having to go to other sources of material. You learn as you go! Its the easiest way to pass an exam.

HUMOR

Studying can be tedious and dry. MznLnx's instructional design includes moderate humor within the exam questions on occassion, to break the tedium and revitalize the brain

Chapter 1. REFERENCE: FRACTIONS, DECIMALS, PERCENTS, GEOMETRY, AND STUDY SKILLS

1. In mathematics, _____ is the decomposition of an object into a product of other objects, or factors, which when multiplied together give the original.
   a. Thing
   b. Factoring0
   c. Undefined
   d. Undefined

2. _____, in number theory is the process of breaking down a composite number into smaller non-trivial divisors, which when multiplied together equal the original integer.
   a. Integer factorization0
   b. Thing
   c. Undefined
   d. Undefined

3. _____ is a branch of mathematics concerning the study of structure, relation and quantity.
   a. Concept
   b. Algebra0
   c. Undefined
   d. Undefined

4. In mathematics, a _____ number (or a _____) is a natural number that has exactly two (distinct) natural number divisors, which are 1 and the _____ number itself.
   a. Prime0
   b. Thing
   c. Undefined
   d. Undefined

5. In mathematics, a _____ can mean either an element of the set {1, 2, 3, ...} (i.e the positive integers or the counting numbers) or an element of the set {0, 1, 2, 3, ...} (i.e. the non-negative integers).
   a. Thing
   b. Natural number0
   c. Undefined
   d. Undefined

6. The _____ of measurement are a globally standardized and modernized form of the metric system.
   a. Thing
   b. Units0
   c. Undefined
   d. Undefined

7. _____ is the mathematical action of repeatedly adding or subtracting one, usually to find out how many objects there are or to set aside a desired number of objects.
   a. Counting0
   b. Thing
   c. Undefined
   d. Undefined

8. In mathematics, a _____ can mean either an element of the set {1, 2, 3, ...} (i.e the positive integers) or an element of the set {0, 1, 2, 3, ...} (i.e. the non-negative integers).
   a. Whole number0
   b. Concept
   c. Undefined
   d. Undefined

9. A _____ is a numeral used to indicate a count. The most common use of the word today is to name the part of a fraction that tells the number or count of equal parts.
   a. Numerator0
   b. Thing
   c. Undefined
   d. Undefined

10. A _____ is the part of a fraction that tells how many equal parts make up a whole, and which is used in the name of the fraction: "halves", "thirds", "fourths" or "quarters", "fifths" and so on.

Chapter 1. REFERENCE: FRACTIONS, DECIMALS, PERCENTS, GEOMETRY, AND STUDY SKILLS

a. Denominator0
b. Concept
c. Undefined
d. Undefined

11. A _____ fraction is a fraction in which the absolute value of the numerator is less than the denominator--hence, the absolute value of the fraction is less than 1.
    a. Proper0
    b. Thing
    c. Undefined
    d. Undefined

12. In mathematics, an inequality is a statement about the relative size or order of two objects. For example 14 > 10, or 14 is _____ 10.
    a. Greater than0
    b. Thing
    c. Undefined
    d. Undefined

13. A _____ is the sum of a whole number and a proper fraction.
    a. Thing
    b. Mixed number0
    c. Undefined
    d. Undefined

14. In mathematics, a _____ is the result of multiplying, or an expression that identifies factors to be multiplied.
    a. Thing
    b. Product0
    c. Undefined
    d. Undefined

15. In mathematics, factorization (British English: factorisation) or factoring is the decomposition of an object (for example, a number, a polynomial, or a matrix) into a product of other objects, or _____, which when multiplied together give the original.
    a. Thing
    b. Factors0
    c. Undefined
    d. Undefined

16. The _____ of a positive integer are the prime numbers that divide into that integer exactly, without leaving a remainder. The process of finding these numbers is called integer factorization, or prime factorization.
    a. Thing
    b. Prime factor0
    c. Undefined
    d. Undefined

17. _____ is a natural number that has exactly two distinct natural number divisors, which are 1 and the _____ itself.
    a. Thing
    b. Prime number0
    c. Undefined
    d. Undefined

18. A frame of _____ is a particular perspective from which the universe is observed.
    a. Thing
    b. Reference0
    c. Undefined
    d. Undefined

19. _____ is a way of expressing a number as a fraction of 100 per cent meaning "per hundred".
    a. Thing
    b. Percent0
    c. Undefined
    d. Undefined

20. _____ is the largest positive integer that divides both numbers without remainder.

Chapter 1. REFERENCE: FRACTIONS, DECIMALS, PERCENTS, GEOMETRY, AND STUDY SKILLS

a. Common Factor0
c. Undefined
b. Thing
d. Undefined

21. In mathematics, a _____ of an integer n, also called a factor of n, is an integer which evenly divides n without leaving a remainder.
    a. Thing
    b. Divisor0
    c. Undefined
    d. Undefined

22. Equivalence is the condition of being _____ or essentially equal.
    a. Equivalent0
    b. Thing
    c. Undefined
    d. Undefined

23. In botany, _____ are above-ground plant organs specialized for photosynthesis. Their characteristics are typically analyzed by using Fiobonacci's sequences.
    a. Leaves0
    b. Thing
    c. Undefined
    d. Undefined

24. In mathematics, the multiplicative inverse of a number x, denoted 1/x or x^{-1}, is the number which, when multiplied by x, yields 1. The multiplicative inverse of x is also called the _____ of x.
    a. Reciprocal0
    b. Thing
    c. Undefined
    d. Undefined

25. A _____ of a number is the product of that number with any integer.
    a. Multiple0
    b. Thing
    c. Undefined
    d. Undefined

26. The _____ of two integers is the smallest positive integer that is a multiple of both intergers.
    a. Thing
    b. Least common multiple0
    c. Undefined
    d. Undefined

27. A _____ is the result of the addition of a set of numbers. The numbers may be natural numbers, complex numbers, matrices, or still more complicated objects. An infinite _____ is a subtle procedure known as a series.
    a. Thing
    b. Sum0
    c. Undefined
    d. Undefined

28. The mathematical concept of a _____ expresses the intuitive idea of deterministic dependence between two quantities, one of which is viewed as primary and the other as secondary. A _____ then is a way to associate a unique output for each input of a specified type, for example, a real number or an element of a given set.
    a. Thing
    b. Function0
    c. Undefined
    d. Undefined

29. In common philosophical language, a proposition or _____, is the content of an assertion, that is, it is true-or-false and defined by the meaning of a particular piece of language.
    a. Statement0
    b. Concept
    c. Undefined
    d. Undefined

Chapter 1. REFERENCE: FRACTIONS, DECIMALS, PERCENTS, GEOMETRY, AND STUDY SKILLS

30. A _____ is a function that assigns a number to subsets of a given set.
    a. Thing
    b. Measure0
    c. Undefined
    d. Undefined

31. A _____ is a unit of length, usually used to measure distance, in a number of different systems, including Imperial units, United States customary units and Norwegian/Swedish mil. Its size can vary from system to system, but in each is between 1 and 10 kilometers. In contemporary English contexts _____ refers to either:
    a. Thing
    b. Mile0
    c. Undefined
    d. Undefined

32. In mathematics, an _____, mean, or central tendency of a data set refers to a measure of the "middle" or "expected" value of the data set.
    a. Concept
    b. Average0
    c. Undefined
    d. Undefined

33. _____ is the distance around a given two-dimensional object. As a general rule, the _____ of a polygon can always be calculated by adding all the length of the sides together. So, the formula for triangles is P = a + b + c, where a, b and c stand for each side of it. For quadrilaterals the equation is P = a + b + c + d. For equilateral polygons, P = na, where n is the number of sides and a is the side length.
    a. Thing
    b. Perimeter0
    c. Undefined
    d. Undefined

34. _____ is a set of numbers, in the broadest sense of the word, together with one or more operations, such as addition or multiplication.
    a. Thing
    b. Number system0
    c. Undefined
    d. Undefined

35. A _____ is a symbol or group of symbols, or a word in a natural language that represents a number.
    a. Numeral0
    b. Thing
    c. Undefined
    d. Undefined

36. The decimal separator is a symbol used to mark the boundary between the integral and the fractional parts of a decimal numeral. Terms implying the symbol used are _____ and decimal comma.
    a. Decimal point0
    b. Concept
    c. Undefined
    d. Undefined

37. _____ is a numeral system in which each position is related to the next by a constant multiplier, a common ratio, called the base or radix of that numeral system.
    a. Thing
    b. Place value0
    c. Undefined
    d. Undefined

38. A _____ number is a positive integer which has a positive divisor other than one or itself.
    a. Composite0
    b. Thing
    c. Undefined
    d. Undefined

39. A _____ decimal is a decimal fraction which ends after a definite number of digits.

Chapter 1. REFERENCE: FRACTIONS, DECIMALS, PERCENTS, GEOMETRY, AND STUDY SKILLS

a. Thing
b. Terminating0
c. Undefined
d. Undefined

40. A _____ decimal is a number whose decimal representation eventually becomes periodic (i.e. the same number sequence _____ indefinitely).
   a. Repeating0
   b. Thing
   c. Undefined
   d. Undefined

41. _____ represent rational numbers whose fractions in lowest terms are of the form $k/(2^n 5^m)$.
   a. Thing
   b. Terminating Decimals0
   c. Undefined
   d. Undefined

42. Recurring or _____ are numbers which when expressed as decimals have a set of "final" digits which repeat an infinite number of times.
   a. Thing
   b. Repeating decimals0
   c. Undefined
   d. Undefined

43. A _____ is a consumption tax charged at the point of purchase for certain goods and services.
   a. Thing
   b. Sales tax0
   c. Undefined
   d. Undefined

44. The _____, the average in everyday English, which is also called the arithmetic _____ (and is distinguished from the geometric _____ or harmonic _____). The average is also called the sample _____. The expected value of a random variable, which is also called the population _____.
   a. Mean0
   b. Thing
   c. Undefined
   d. Undefined

45. In mathematics, _____ is an elementary arithmetic operation. When one of the numbers is a whole number, _____ is the repeated sum of the other number.
   a. Thing
   b. Multiplication0
   c. Undefined
   d. Undefined

46. _____ is a kind of property which exists as magnitude or multitude. It is among the basic classes of things along with quality, substance, change, and relation.
   a. Amount0
   b. Thing
   c. Undefined
   d. Undefined

47. A _____ is a deliberate process for transforming one or more inputs into one or more results.
   a. Calculation0
   b. Thing
   c. Undefined
   d. Undefined

48. In finance and economics, _____ is the process of finding the present value of an amount of cash at some future date, and along with compounding cash forms the basis of time value of money calculations.
   a. Thing
   b. Discount0
   c. Undefined
   d. Undefined

Chapter 1. REFERENCE: FRACTIONS, DECIMALS, PERCENTS, GEOMETRY, AND STUDY SKILLS

49. _____ is a form of periodic payment from an employer to an employee, which is specified in an employment contract.
    a. Thing
    b. Gross pay0
    c. Undefined
    d. Undefined

50. A _____ is a form of periodic payment from an employer to an employee, which is specified in an employment contract.
    a. Thing
    b. Salary0
    c. Undefined
    d. Undefined

51. In set theory and other branches of mathematics, the _____ of a collection of sets is the set that contains everything that belongs to any of the sets, but nothing else.
    a. Union0
    b. Thing
    c. Undefined
    d. Undefined

52. _____ is the level of functional and/or metabolic efficiency of an organism at both the micro level.
    a. Health0
    b. Thing
    c. Undefined
    d. Undefined

53. _____ is the fee paid on borrowed money.
    a. Thing
    b. Interest0
    c. Undefined
    d. Undefined

54. A _____ are accounts maintained by commercial banks, savings and loan associations, credit unions, and mutual savings banks that pay interest but can not be used directly as money by, for example, writing a cheque.
    a. Thing
    b. Savings account0
    c. Undefined
    d. Undefined

55. In economics _____ means before deductions brutto, e.g. _____ domestic or national product, or _____ profit or income
    a. Thing
    b. Gross0
    c. Undefined
    d. Undefined

56. _____ primarily refers to social welfare service concerned with social protection, or protection against socially recognized conditions, including poverty, old age, disability, unemployment, families with children and others.
    a. Social security0
    b. Thing
    c. Undefined
    d. Undefined

57. In topology and related areas of mathematics a _____ or Moore-Smith sequence is a generalization of a sequence, intended to unify the various notions of limit and generalize them to arbitrary topological spaces.
    a. Thing
    b. Net0
    c. Undefined
    d. Undefined

58. A _____ or CD is a time deposit, a financial product commonly offered to consumers by banks, thrift institutions, and credit unions.

Chapter 1. REFERENCE: FRACTIONS, DECIMALS, PERCENTS, GEOMETRY, AND STUDY SKILLS

a. Thing
c. Undefined
b. Certificate of deposit0
d. Undefined

59. A _____ is a method of using property as security for the payment of a debt.
a. Thing
c. Undefined
b. Mortgage0
d. Undefined

60. Acid _____ ratio measures the ability of a company to use its near cash or quick assets to immediately extinguish its current liabilities.
a. Thing
c. Undefined
b. Test0
d. Undefined

61. _____ are external two-dimensional outlines, with the appearance or configuration of some thing - in contrast to the matter or content or substance of which it is composed.
a. Shapes0
c. Undefined
b. Thing
d. Undefined

62. _____ is the estimation of a physical quantity such as distance, energy, temperature, or time.
a. Thing
c. Undefined
b. Measurement0
d. Undefined

63. The _____ is the distance around a closed curve. _____ is a kind of perimeter.
a. Circumference0
c. Undefined
b. Thing
d. Undefined

64. In plane geometry, a _____ is a polygon with four equal sides, four right angles, and parallel opposite sides. In algebra, the _____ of a number is that number multiplied by itself.
a. Thing
c. Undefined
b. Square0
d. Undefined

65. _____ are any documents that aim to streamline particular processes according to a set routine.
a. Guidelines0
c. Undefined
b. Thing
d. Undefined

66. _____ or arithmetics is the oldest and most elementary branch of mathematics, used by almost everyone, for tasks ranging from simple daily counting to advanced science and business calculations.
a. Thing
c. Undefined
b. Arithmetic0
d. Undefined

67. In arithmetic and algebra, when a number or expression is both preceded and followed by a binary operation, an _____ is required for which operation should be applied first.
a. Order of operations0
c. Undefined
b. Thing
d. Undefined

68. _____, either of the curved-bracket punctuation marks that together make a set of _____

Chapter 1. REFERENCE: FRACTIONS, DECIMALS, PERCENTS, GEOMETRY, AND STUDY SKILLS

a. Thing
b. Parentheses0
c. Undefined
d. Undefined

69. In Euclidean geometry, a _____ is the set of all points in a plane at a fixed distance, called the radius, from a given point, the center.
a. Thing
b. Circle0
c. Undefined
d. Undefined

70. In classical geometry, a _____ of a circle or sphere is any line segment from its center to its boundary. By extension, the _____ of a circle or sphere is the length of any such segment. The _____ is half the diameter. In science and engineering the term _____ of curvature is commonly used as a synonym for _____.
a. Radius0
b. Thing
c. Undefined
d. Undefined

71. The _____ of a solid object is the three-dimensional concept of how much space it occupies, often quantified numerically.
a. Volume0
b. Thing
c. Undefined
d. Undefined

72. In mathematics, _____ geometry was the traditional name for the geometry of three-dimensional Euclidean space — for practical purposes the kind of space we live in.
a. Thing
b. Solid0
c. Undefined
d. Undefined

73. _____ are cubes in which all sides are of the same length and all face perpendicular to each other including an atom at each corner of the unigt cell.
a. Cubic units0
b. Thing
c. Undefined
d. Undefined

74. In mathematics, a _____ is a quadric surface, with the following equation in Cartesian coordinates: $(x/_a)^2 + (y/_b)^2 = 1$.
a. Thing
b. Cylinder0
c. Undefined
d. Undefined

75. _____ is a branch of mathematics which deals with triangles, particularly triangles in a plane where one angle of the triangle is 90 degrees, and a variety of other topological relations such as spheres, in other branches, such as spherical _____.
a. Trigonometry0
b. Thing
c. Undefined
d. Undefined

76. _____ is a mathematical subject that includes the study of limits, derivatives, integrals, and power series and constitutes a major part of modern university curriculum.
a. Thing
b. Calculus0
c. Undefined
d. Undefined

Chapter 1. REFERENCE: FRACTIONS, DECIMALS, PERCENTS, GEOMETRY, AND STUDY SKILLS

77. In geometry, a _____ is a special kind of point, usually a corner of a polygon, polyhedron, or higher dimensional polytope. In the geometry of curves a _____ is a point of where the first derivative of curvature is zero. In graph theory, a _____ is the fundamental unit out of which graphs are formed
   a. Thing
   b. Vertex0
   c. Undefined
   d. Undefined

78. An angle equal to two right angles is called a _____ (equal to 180 degrees).
   a. Straight angle0
   b. Thing
   c. Undefined
   d. Undefined

79. In geometry and trigonometry, a _____ is defined as an angle between two straight intersecting lines of ninety degrees, or one-quarter of a circle.
   a. Thing
   b. Right angle0
   c. Undefined
   d. Undefined

80. In mathematics, there are several meanings of _____ depending on the subject.
   a. Degree0
   b. Thing
   c. Undefined
   d. Undefined

81. Angles smaller than a right angle are called _____ angles (less than 90 degrees).
   a. Concept
   b. Acute0
   c. Undefined
   d. Undefined

82. Any angle larger than 90 degrees and less than 180 degrees, is called an _____ angle.
   a. Obtuse0
   b. Concept
   c. Undefined
   d. Undefined

83. In geometry, two sets are called _____ if one can be transformed into the other by an isometry, i.e., a combination of translations, rotations and reflections.
   a. Thing
   b. Congruent0
   c. Undefined
   d. Undefined

84. A pair of angles are said to be _____ if they share the same vertex and are bounded by the same pair of lines but are opposite to each other. They are also congruent.
   a. Vertical angles0
   b. Thing
   c. Undefined
   d. Undefined

85. The existence and properties of _____ are the basis of Euclid's parallel postulate. _____ are two lines on the same plane that do not intersect even assuming that lines extend to infinity in either direction.
   a. Parallel lines0
   b. Thing
   c. Undefined
   d. Undefined

86. In mathematics, a _____ is a two-dimensional manifold or surface that is perfectly flat.
   a. Thing
   b. Plane0
   c. Undefined
   d. Undefined

Chapter 1. REFERENCE: FRACTIONS, DECIMALS, PERCENTS, GEOMETRY, AND STUDY SKILLS

87. In combinatorial mathematics, given a collection C of disjoint sets, a _____ is a set containing exactly one element from each member of the collection: it is a section of the quotient map induced by the collection.
    a. Thing
    b. Transversal0
    c. Undefined
    d. Undefined

88. In mathematics, the conjugate _____ or adjoint matrix of an m-by-n matrix A with complex entries is the n-by-m matrix A* obtained from A by taking the transpose and then taking the complex conjugate of each entry.
    a. Pairs0
    b. Thing
    c. Undefined
    d. Undefined

89. A _____ is one of the basic shapes of geometry: a polygon with three vertices and three sides which are straight line segments.
    a. Triangle0
    b. Thing
    c. Undefined
    d. Undefined

90. An _____ has internal angles that are all smaller than 90° (three acute angles).
    a. Thing
    b. Acute triangle0
    c. Undefined
    d. Undefined

91. _____ has one 90° internal angle a right angle.
    a. Thing
    b. Right triangle0
    c. Undefined
    d. Undefined

92. An _____ is a triangle that has one internal angle larger than 90°
    a. Obtuse triangle0
    b. Thing
    c. Undefined
    d. Undefined

93. In geometry, an _____ polygon is a polygon which has all sides of the same length.
    a. Thing
    b. Equilateral0
    c. Undefined
    d. Undefined

94. An _____ is a triangle in which all sides are of equal length.
    a. Thing
    b. Equilateral triangle0
    c. Undefined
    d. Undefined

95. In mathematics, the additive inverse, or _____ of a number n is the number that, when added to n, yields zero. The additive inverse of n is denoted −n. For example, 7 is −7, because 7 + (−7) = 0, and the additive inverse of −0.3 is 0.3, because −0.3 + 0.3 = 0.
    a. Thing
    b. Opposite0
    c. Undefined
    d. Undefined

96. In a _____ triangle, all sides have different lengths. The internal angles in a _____ triangle are all different.
    a. Scalene0
    b. Thing
    c. Undefined
    d. Undefined

97. In a _____ all sides have different lengths. The internal angles in a _____ are all different..

Chapter 1. REFERENCE: FRACTIONS, DECIMALS, PERCENTS, GEOMETRY, AND STUDY SKILLS

a. Scalene triangle0
b. Thing
c. Undefined
d. Undefined

98. An _____ triange is a triangle with at least two sides of equal length.
a. Thing
b. Isosceles0
c. Undefined
d. Undefined

99. In mathematics, the _____ of a number n is the number that, when added to n, yields zero. The _____ of n is denoted −n. For example, 7 is −7, because 7 + (−7) = 0, and the _____ of −0.3 is 0.3, because −0.3 + 0.3 = 0.
a. Thing
b. Additive inverse0
c. Undefined
d. Undefined

100. A _____ is a simplified and structured visual representation of concepts, ideas, constructions, relations, statistical data, anatomy etc used in all aspects of human activities to visualize and clarify the topic.
a. Diagram0
b. Thing
c. Undefined
d. Undefined

101. A pair of angles is _____ if their respective measures sum to 180 degrees.
a. Concept
b. Supplementary0
c. Undefined
d. Undefined

102. A _____ is a unit of length in the metric system, equal to one thousand metres, the current SI base unit of length
a. Kilometer0
b. Thing
c. Undefined
d. Undefined

103. _____ is a three-dimensional geometric shape formed by straight lines through a fixed point vertex to the points of a fixed curve directrix.
a. Thing
b. Right circular cone0
c. Undefined
d. Undefined

104. A _____ is a three-dimensional geometric shape formed by straight lines through a fixed point (vertex) to the points of a fixed curve (directrix)
a. Cone0
b. Concept
c. Undefined
d. Undefined

105. A _____ is a three-dimensional solid object bounded by six square faces, facets, or sides, with three meeting at each vertex.
a. Thing
b. Cube0
c. Undefined
d. Undefined

106. A pair of angles are _____ if the sum of their angles is 90°.
a. Complementary0
b. Concept
c. Undefined
d. Undefined

107. An _____ is an angle formed by two sides of a simple polygon that share an endpoint, namely, the angle on the inner side of the polygon.

Chapter 1. REFERENCE: FRACTIONS, DECIMALS, PERCENTS, GEOMETRY, AND STUDY SKILLS

a. Interior angle0
b. Thing
c. Undefined
d. Undefined

108. In set theory and other branches of mathematics, two kinds of complements are defined, the relative _____ and the absolute _____.
 a. Thing
 b. Complement0
 c. Undefined
 d. Undefined

109. A _____ is a quadrilateral, which is defined as a shape with four sides, which has a pair of parallel sides.
 a. Thing
 b. Trapezoid0
 c. Undefined
 d. Undefined

110. In geometry, a _____ is defined as a quadrilateral where all four of its angles are right angles.
 a. Rectangle0
 b. Thing
 c. Undefined
 d. Undefined

111. In mathematics, a _____ is the set of all points in three-dimensional space (R^3) which are at distance r from a fixed point of that space, where r is a positive real number called the radius of the _____. The fixed point is called the center or centre, and is not part of the _____ itself.
 a. Thing
 b. Sphere0
 c. Undefined
 d. Undefined

112. A _____ is a four-sided plane figure that has two sets of opposite parallel sides.
 a. Concept
 b. Parallelogram0
 c. Undefined
 d. Undefined

113. In geometry a _____ is a plane figure that is bounded by a closed path or circuit, composed of a finite number of sequential line segments.
 a. Thing
 b. Polygon0
 c. Undefined
 d. Undefined

114. In _____ algebra, a *-ring is an associative ring with an antilinear, antiautomorphism * : A ¨ A which is an involution.
 a. Star0
 b. Thing
 c. Undefined
 d. Undefined

Chapter 2. SET OF REAL NUMBERS

1. A _____ is a one-dimensional picture in which the integers are shown as specially-marked points evenly spaced on a line.
   - a. Thing
   - b. Number line0
   - c. Undefined
   - d. Undefined

2. In mathematics, a _____ may be described informally as a number that can be given by an infinite decimal representation.
   - a. Thing
   - b. Real number0
   - c. Undefined
   - d. Undefined

3. A _____ is a number that is less than zero.
   - a. Negative number0
   - b. Thing
   - c. Undefined
   - d. Undefined

4. In mathematics, the additive inverse, or _____ of a number n is the number that, when added to n, yields zero. The additive inverse of n is denoted −n. For example, 7 is −7, because 7 + (−7) = 0, and the additive inverse of −0.3 is 0.3, because −0.3 + 0.3 = 0.
   - a. Opposite0
   - b. Thing
   - c. Undefined
   - d. Undefined

5. In astronomy, geography, geometry and related sciences and contexts, a plane is said to be _____ at a given point if it is locally perpendicular to the gradient of the gravity field, i.e., with the direction of the gravitational force at that point.
   - a. Horizontal0
   - b. Thing
   - c. Undefined
   - d. Undefined

6. In mathematics, the _____ (or modulus) of a real number is its numerical value without regard to its sign.
   - a. Absolute value0
   - b. Thing
   - c. Undefined
   - d. Undefined

7. In mathematics, the _____ of a number n is the number that, when added to n, yields zero. The _____ of n is denoted −n. For example, 7 is −7, because 7 + (−7) = 0, and the _____ of −0.3 is 0.3, because −0.3 + 0.3 = 0.
   - a. Additive inverse0
   - b. Thing
   - c. Undefined
   - d. Undefined

8. The _____ of measurement are a globally standardized and modernized form of the metric system.
   - a. Units0
   - b. Thing
   - c. Undefined
   - d. Undefined

9. An _____ or member of a set is an object that when collected together make up the set.
   - a. Thing
   - b. Element0
   - c. Undefined
   - d. Undefined

10. In mathematics, the _____ , or members of a set or more generally a class are all those objects which when collected together make up the set or class.
    - a. Elements0
    - b. Thing
    - c. Undefined
    - d. Undefined

Chapter 2. SET OF REAL NUMBERS

11. _____ are objects, characters, or other concrete representations of ideas, concepts, or other abstractions.
    a. Symbols0
    b. Thing
    c. Undefined
    d. Undefined

12. A _____ is a set whose members are members of another set or a set contained within another set.
    a. Thing
    b. Subset0
    c. Undefined
    d. Undefined

13. _____ are groups whose members are members of another set or a set contained within another set.
    a. Subsets0
    b. Thing
    c. Undefined
    d. Undefined

14. _____ is a branch of mathematics concerning the study of structure, relation and quantity.
    a. Algebra0
    b. Concept
    c. Undefined
    d. Undefined

15. In mathematics, a _____ can mean either an element of the set {1, 2, 3, ...} (i.e the positive integers or the counting numbers) or an element of the set {0, 1, 2, 3, ...} (i.e. the non-negative integers).
    a. Thing
    b. Natural number0
    c. Undefined
    d. Undefined

16. In mathematics, a _____ can mean either an element of the set {1, 2, 3, ...} (i.e the positive integers) or an element of the set {0, 1, 2, 3, ...} (i.e. the non-negative integers).
    a. Concept
    b. Whole number0
    c. Undefined
    d. Undefined

17. The _____ are the only integral domain whose positive elements are well-ordered, and in which order is preserved by addition. Like the natural numbers, the _____ form a countably infinite set. The set of all _____ is usually denoted in mathematics by a boldface Z.
    a. Integers0
    b. Thing
    c. Undefined
    d. Undefined

18. A _____ is a numeral used to indicate a count. The most common use of the word today is to name the part of a fraction that tells the number or count of equal parts.
    a. Numerator0
    b. Thing
    c. Undefined
    d. Undefined

19. In mathematics, a _____ number is a number which can be expressed as a ratio of two integers. Non-integer _____ numbers (commonly called fractions) are usually written as the vulgar fraction a / b, where b is not zero.
    a. Rational0
    b. Thing
    c. Undefined
    d. Undefined

20. A _____ is the part of a fraction that tells how many equal parts make up a whole, and which is used in the name of the fraction: "halves", "thirds", "fourths" or "quarters", "fifths" and so on.

Chapter 2. SET OF REAL NUMBERS

a. Denominator0
b. Concept
c. Undefined
d. Undefined

21. A _____ is a quantity that denotes the proportional amount or magnitude of one quantity relative to another.
   a. Thing
   b. Ratio0
   c. Undefined
   d. Undefined

22. A _____ decimal is a number whose decimal representation eventually becomes periodic (i.e. the same number sequence _____ indefinitely).
   a. Repeating0
   b. Thing
   c. Undefined
   d. Undefined

23. A _____ decimal is a decimal fraction which ends after a definite number of digits.
   a. Thing
   b. Terminating0
   c. Undefined
   d. Undefined

24. A _____ decimal is a decimal for which there is no digit to the right of the decimal point, as all digits farther from the right are zero.
   a. Nonterminating0
   b. Thing
   c. Undefined
   d. Undefined

25. In mathematics, an _____ number is any real number that is not a rational number- that is, it is a number which cannot be expressed as a fraction m/n, where m and n are integers.
   a. Thing
   b. Irrational0
   c. Undefined
   d. Undefined

26. In mathematics, an _____ is any real number that is not a rational number ¡ª that is, it is a number which cannot be expressed as m/n, where m and n are integers.
   a. Thing
   b. Irrational number0
   c. Undefined
   d. Undefined

27. In mathematics, _____ are any real number that is not a rational number ¡ª that is, it is a number which cannot be expressed as m/n, where m and n are integers.
   a. Thing
   b. Irrational numbers0
   c. Undefined
   d. Undefined

28. In mathematics, an _____ is a statement about the relative size or order of two objects.
   a. Thing
   b. Inequality0
   c. Undefined
   d. Undefined

29. In mathematics, an inequality is a statement about the relative size or order of two objects. For example 14 > 10, or 14 is _____ 10.
   a. Greater than0
   b. Thing
   c. Undefined
   d. Undefined

30. An _____ is a combination of numbers, operators, grouping symbols and/or free variables and bound variables arranged in a meaningful way which can be evaluated..
   a. Thing
   b. Expression0
   c. Undefined
   d. Undefined

31. _____ is a physical property of a system that underlies the common notions of hot and cold; something that is hotter has the greater _____.
   a. Temperature0
   b. Thing
   c. Undefined
   d. Undefined

32. The _____ integers are all the integers from zero on upwards.
   a. Nonnegative0
   b. Thing
   c. Undefined
   d. Undefined

33. _____ represent rational numbers whose fractions in lowest terms are of the form $k/(2^n 5^m)$.
   a. Thing
   b. Terminating Decimals0
   c. Undefined
   d. Undefined

34. The _____ of a geographic location is its height above a fixed reference point, often the mean sea level.
   a. Thing
   b. Elevation0
   c. Undefined
   d. Undefined

35. _____ is the largest city in the state of Texas and the fourth-largest in the United States. As of the 2005 U.S. Census estimate, it had a population of more than 2 million.
   a. Houston0
   b. Thing
   c. Undefined
   d. Undefined

36. A _____ is a symbolic representation denoting a quantity or expression. It often represents an "unknown" quantity that has the potential to change.
   a. Thing
   b. Variable0
   c. Undefined
   d. Undefined

37. In Euclidean geometry, a _____ is moving every point a constant distance in a specified direction.
   a. Concept
   b. Translation0
   c. Undefined
   d. Undefined

38. In plane geometry, a _____ is a polygon with four equal sides, four right angles, and parallel opposite sides. In algebra, the _____ of a number is that number multiplied by itself.
   a. Thing
   b. Square0
   c. Undefined
   d. Undefined

39. In mathematics, a _____ of a number x is a number r such that $r^2 = x$, or in words, a number r whose square (the result of multiplying the number by itself) is x.
   a. Square root0
   b. Thing
   c. Undefined
   d. Undefined

Chapter 2. SET OF REAL NUMBERS

40. In arithmetic and algebra, when a number or expression is both preceded and followed by a binary operation, an _____ is required for which operation should be applied first.
    a. Order of operations0
    b. Thing
    c. Undefined
    d. Undefined

41. In mathematics, _____ growth occurs when the growth rate of a function is always proportional to the function's current size.
    a. Thing
    b. Exponential0
    c. Undefined
    d. Undefined

42. In mathematics, a _____ of a complex-valued function f is a member x of the domain of f such that f(x) vanishes at x, that is, x : f (x) = 0.
    a. Thing
    b. Root0
    c. Undefined
    d. Undefined

43. _____, either of the curved-bracket punctuation marks that together make a set of _____
    a. Thing
    b. Parentheses0
    c. Undefined
    d. Undefined

44. In mathematics, _____ is an elementary arithmetic operation. When one of the numbers is a whole number, _____ is the repeated sum of the other number.
    a. Thing
    b. Multiplication0
    c. Undefined
    d. Undefined

45. _____ is a mathematical operation, written a^n, involving two numbers, the base a and the exponent n.
    a. Thing
    b. Exponentiating0
    c. Undefined
    d. Undefined

46. _____ is a mathematical operation, written a^n, involving two numbers, the base a and the exponent n.
    a. Thing
    b. Exponentiation0
    c. Undefined
    d. Undefined

47. _____ has many meanings, most of which simply .
    a. Thing
    b. Power0
    c. Undefined
    d. Undefined

48. In mathematics, factorization (British English: factorisation) or factoring is the decomposition of an object (for example, a number, a polynomial, or a matrix) into a product of other objects, or _____, which when multiplied together give the original.
    a. Factors0
    b. Thing
    c. Undefined
    d. Undefined

49. A _____ is a three-dimensional solid object bounded by six square faces, facets, or sides, with three meeting at each vertex.

Chapter 2. SET OF REAL NUMBERS

a. Cube0
b. Thing
c. Undefined
d. Undefined

50. _____ is the symbol used to indicate the nth root of a number
   a. Radical0
   b. Thing
   c. Undefined
   d. Undefined

51. A _____ fraction is a fraction in which the absolute value of the numerator is less than the denominator--hence, the absolute value of the fraction is less than 1.
   a. Thing
   b. Proper0
   c. Undefined
   d. Undefined

52. In abstract algebra, _____ consists of sets with binary operations that satisfy certain axioms.
   a. Grouping0
   b. Thing
   c. Undefined
   d. Undefined

53. In mathematics, _____ are used to indicate the square root of a number.
   a. Thing
   b. Radicals0
   c. Undefined
   d. Undefined

54. In financial mathematics, the _____ volatility of an option contract is the volatility _____ by the market price of the option based on an option pricing model.
   a. Thing
   b. Implied0
   c. Undefined
   d. Undefined

55. The _____ (symbol _____) and the millibar (symbol mbar, also mb) are units of pressure.
   a. Thing
   b. Bar0
   c. Undefined
   d. Undefined

56. In mathematics, the multiplicative inverse of a number x, denoted 1/x or x^{-1}, is the number which, when multiplied by x, yields 1. The multiplicative inverse of x is also called the _____ of x.
   a. Thing
   b. Reciprocal0
   c. Undefined
   d. Undefined

57. A _____ is the result of the addition of a set of numbers. The numbers may be natural numbers, complex numbers, matrices, or still more complicated objects. An infinite _____ is a subtle procedure known as a series.
   a. Thing
   b. Sum0
   c. Undefined
   d. Undefined

58. In geometry, a _____ is defined as a quadrilateral where all four of its angles are right angles.
   a. Thing
   b. Rectangle0
   c. Undefined
   d. Undefined

Chapter 2. SET OF REAL NUMBERS

59. _____ is the distance around a given two-dimensional object. As a general rule, the _____ of a polygon can always be calculated by adding all the length of the sides together. So, the formula for triangles is P = a + b + c, where a, b and c stand for each side of it. For quadrilaterals the equation is P = a + b + c + d. For equilateral polygons, P = na, where n is the number of sides and a is the side length.
   a. Thing
   b. Perimeter0
   c. Undefined
   d. Undefined

60. A _____ is a quadrilateral, which is defined as a shape with four sides, which has a pair of parallel sides.
   a. Thing
   b. Trapezoid0
   c. Undefined
   d. Undefined

61. The _____ of an algebraic expression is the same equation, but without parentheses.
   a. Thing
   b. Expanded form0
   c. Undefined
   d. Undefined

62. In mathematics, a _____ is the result of multiplying, or an expression that identifies factors to be multiplied.
   a. Product0
   b. Thing
   c. Undefined
   d. Undefined

63. In mathematics, a _____ is the end result of a division problem. It can also be expressed as the number of times the divisor divides into the dividend.
   a. Thing
   b. Quotient0
   c. Undefined
   d. Undefined

64. _____ is the mathematical action of repeatedly adding or subtracting one, usually to find out how many objects there are or to set aside a desired number of objects.
   a. Thing
   b. Counting0
   c. Undefined
   d. Undefined

65. A _____ is a negotiable instrument instructing a financial institution to pay a specific amount of a specific currency from a specific demand account held in the maker/depositor's name with that institution. Both the maker and payee may be natural persons or legal entities.
   a. Check0
   b. Thing
   c. Undefined
   d. Undefined

66. _____ is a state located in the Midwestern region of the United States of America.
   a. Thing
   b. Minnesota0
   c. Undefined
   d. Undefined

67. The _____ rule, also known as a slipstick, is a mechanical analog computer, consisting of at least two finely divided scales , most often a fixed outer pair and a movable inner one, with a sliding window called the cursor.
   a. Slide0
   b. Thing
   c. Undefined
   d. Undefined

68. A _____ is one of the basic shapes of geometry: a polygon with three vertices and three sides which are straight line segments.

Chapter 2. SET OF REAL NUMBERS

a. Thing
c. Undefined
b. Triangle0
d. Undefined

69. A _____ is a landform that extends above the surrounding terrain in a limited area. A _____ is generally steeper than a hill, but there is no universally accepted standard definition for the height of a _____ or a hill although a _____ usually has an identifiable summit.
a. Thing
c. Undefined
b. Mountain0
d. Undefined

70. The plus and _____ signs are mathematical symbols used to represent the notions of positive and negative as well as the operations of addition and subtraction.
a. Thing
c. Undefined
b. Minus0
d. Undefined

71. The metre (or _____, see spelling differences) is a measure of length. It is the basic unit of length in the metric system and in the International System of Units (SI), used around the world for general and scientific purposes.
a. Meter0
c. Undefined
b. Concept
d. Undefined

72. In mathematics, defined and _____ are used to explain whether or not expressions have meaningful, sensible, and unambiguous values.
a. Undefined0
c. Undefined
b. Thing
d. Undefined

73. A _____ is the sum of a whole number and a proper fraction.
a. Thing
c. Undefined
b. Mixed number0
d. Undefined

74. _____ is, or relates to, the _____ temperature scale .
a. Thing
c. Undefined
b. Celsius0
d. Undefined

75. In mathematics, an _____, mean, or central tendency of a data set refers to a measure of the "middle" or "expected" value of the data set.
a. Concept
c. Undefined
b. Average0
d. Undefined

76. The _____ is a popular form of gambling which involves the drawing of lots for a prize. Some governments forbid it, while others endorse it to the extent of organizign a national _____
a. Thing
c. Undefined
b. Lottery0
d. Undefined

77. In topology and related areas of mathematics a _____ or Moore-Smith sequence is a generalization of a sequence, intended to unify the various notions of limit and generalize them to arbitrary topological spaces.

Chapter 2. SET OF REAL NUMBERS

    a. Net0
    b. Thing
    c. Undefined
    d. Undefined

78. In mathematics, _____ expressions is used to reduce the expression into the lowest possible term.
    a. Simplifying0
    b. Thing
    c. Undefined
    d. Undefined

79. An _____ is an equality that remains true regardless of the values of any variables that appear within it, to distinguish it from an equality which is true under more particular conditions.
    a. Thing
    b. Identity0
    c. Undefined
    d. Undefined

80. In mathematics, and in particular in abstract algebra, the _____ is a property of binary operations that generalises the distributive law from elementary algebra.
    a. Distributive property0
    b. Thing
    c. Undefined
    d. Undefined

81. The _____ is a property of multiplication or addition where the product or sum remains the same, regardless of whether or not the order of the addends or factors are changed.
    a. Thing
    b. Commutative property0
    c. Undefined
    d. Undefined

82. In mathematics, _____ is a property that a binary operation can have. Within an expression containing two or more of the same associative operators in a row, the order of operations does not matter as long as the sequence of the operands is not changed.
    a. Associativity0
    b. Thing
    c. Undefined
    d. Undefined

83. In mathematics, the _____ inverse of a number x, denoted $1/x$ or x^{-1}, is the number which, when multiplied by x, yields 1. The _____ inverse of x is also called the reciprocal of x.
    a. Multiplicative0
    b. Thing
    c. Undefined
    d. Undefined

84. In mathematics, an _____ (or neutral element) is a special type of element of a set with respect to a binary operation on that set.
    a. Concept
    b. Identity element0
    c. Undefined
    d. Undefined

85. _____ element of an element x with respect to a binary operation * with identity element e is an element y such that $x * y = y * x = e$. In particular,
    a. Inverse0
    b. Thing
    c. Undefined
    d. Undefined

86. The _____, the average in everyday English, which is also called the arithmetic _____ (and is distinguished from the geometric _____ or harmonic _____). The average is also called the sample _____. The expected value of a random variable, which is also called the population _____.

a. Mean0
b. Thing
c. Undefined
d. Undefined

87. In mathematics and the mathematical sciences, a _____ is a fixed, but possibly unspecified, value. This is in contrast to a variable, which is not fixed.
   a. Thing
   b. Constant0
   c. Undefined
   d. Undefined

88. In mathematics, a _____ is a constant multiplicative factor of a certain object. The object can be such things as a variable, a vector, a function, etc. For example, the _____ of $9x^2$ is 9.
   a. Thing
   b. Coefficient0
   c. Undefined
   d. Undefined

89. In mathematics, the conjugate _____ or adjoint matrix of an m-by-n matrix A with complex entries is the n-by-m matrix A* obtained from A by taking the transpose and then taking the complex conjugate of each entry.
   a. Pairs0
   b. Thing
   c. Undefined
   d. Undefined

90. In common philosophical language, a proposition or _____, is the content of an assertion, that is, it is true-or-false and defined by the meaning of a particular piece of language.
   a. Concept
   b. Statement0
   c. Undefined
   d. Undefined

91. Equivalence is the condition of being _____ or essentially equal.
   a. Thing
   b. Equivalent0
   c. Undefined
   d. Undefined

92. In mathematics, a _____ is an expression that is constructed from one or more variables and constants, using only the operations of addition, subtraction, multiplication, and constant positive whole number exponents. is a _____. Note in particular that division by an expression containing a variable is not in general allowed in polynomials. [1]
   a. Thing
   b. Polynomial0
   c. Undefined
   d. Undefined

93. _____ was a German mathematician and scientist of profound genius who contributed significantly to many fields, including number theory, analysis, differential geometry, geodesy, magnetism, astronomy, and optics.
   a. Karl Friedrich Gauss0
   b. Person
   c. Undefined
   d. Undefined

94. A _____ is a set of numbers that designate location in a given reference system, such as x,y in a planar _____ system or an x,y,z in a three-dimensional _____ system.
   a. Thing
   b. Coordinate0
   c. Undefined
   d. Undefined

95. In mathematics and its applications, a _____ is a system for assigning an n-tuple of numbers or scalars to each point in an n-dimensional space.

Chapter 2. SET OF REAL NUMBERS

a. Concept
b. Coordinate system0
c. Undefined
d. Undefined

96. In geometry, the _____ of an object is a point in some sense in the middle of the object.
a. Thing
b. Center0
c. Undefined
d. Undefined

97. In geometry and trigonometry, a _____ is defined as an angle between two straight intersecting lines of ninety degrees, or one-quarter of a circle.
a. Right angle0
b. Thing
c. Undefined
d. Undefined

98. In mathematics, the _____ of a coordinate system is the point where the axes of the system intersect.
a. Thing
b. Origin0
c. Undefined
d. Undefined

99. A _____ consists of one quarter of the coordinate plane.
a. Thing
b. Quadrant0
c. Undefined
d. Undefined

100. An _____ is a collection of two not necessarily distinct objects, one of which is distinguished as the first coordinate and the other as the second coordinate.
a. Ordered pair0
b. Thing
c. Undefined
d. Undefined

101. _____ is a temperature scale named after the German physicist Daniel Gabriel _____ , who proposed it in 1724.
a. Thing
b. Fahrenheit0
c. Undefined
d. Undefined

102. In business, particularly accounting, a _____ is the time intervals that the accounts, statement, payments, or other calculations cover.
a. Thing
b. Period0
c. Undefined
d. Undefined

103. In mathematics, a _____ is a two-dimensional manifold or surface that is perfectly flat.
a. Plane0
b. Thing
c. Undefined
d. Undefined

104. _____ is a mathematical science pertaining to the collection, analysis, interpretation or explanation, and presentation of data. It is applicable to a wide variety of academic disciplines, from the physical and social sciences to the humanities.
a. Statistics0
b. Thing
c. Undefined
d. Undefined

105. In mathematics, the concept of a _____ tries to capture the intuitive idea of a geometrical one-dimensional and continuous object. A simple example is the circle.
   a. Curve0
   b. Thing
   c. Undefined
   d. Undefined

106. _____ is a synonym for information.
   a. Data0
   b. Thing
   c. Undefined
   d. Undefined

107. Deductive _____ is the kind of _____ in which the conclusion is necessitated by, or reached from, previously known facts (the premises).
   a. Thing
   b. Reasoning0
   c. Undefined
   d. Undefined

108. A _____ is a unit of length, usually used to measure distance, in a number of different systems, including Imperial units, United States customary units and Norwegian/Swedish mil. Its size can vary from system to system, but in each is between 1 and 10 kilometers. In contemporary English contexts _____ refers to either:
   a. Thing
   b. Mile0
   c. Undefined
   d. Undefined

109. In Euclidean geometry, a _____ is the set of all points in a plane at a fixed distance, called the radius, from a given point, the center.
   a. Circle0
   b. Thing
   c. Undefined
   d. Undefined

110. Compass and straightedge or ruler-and-compass _____ is the _____ of lengths or angles using only an idealized ruler and compass.
   a. Thing
   b. Construction0
   c. Undefined
   d. Undefined

111. _____ is the design, analysis, and/or construction of works for practical purposes.
   a. Engineering0
   b. Thing
   c. Undefined
   d. Undefined

112. The _____ of a mathematical object is its size: a property by which it can be larger or smaller than other objects of the same kind; in technical terms, an ordering of the class of objects to which it belongs.
   a. Magnitude0
   b. Thing
   c. Undefined
   d. Undefined

Chapter 3. LINEAR EQUATIONS AND INEQUALITIES

1. In mathematics, _____ is an elementary arithmetic operation. When one of the numbers is a whole number, _____ is the repeated sum of the other number.
   a. Multiplication0
   b. Thing
   c. Undefined
   d. Undefined

2. A _____ is a symbolic representation denoting a quantity or expression. It often represents an "unknown" quantity that has the potential to change.
   a. Variable0
   b. Thing
   c. Undefined
   d. Undefined

3. Two mathematical objects are equal if and only if they are precisely the same in every way. This defines a binary relation, _____, denoted by the sign of _____ "=" in such a way that the statement "x = y" means that x and y are equal.
   a. Equality0
   b. Thing
   c. Undefined
   d. Undefined

4. In common philosophical language, a proposition or _____, is the content of an assertion, that is, it is true-or-false and defined by the meaning of a particular piece of language.
   a. Statement0
   b. Concept
   c. Undefined
   d. Undefined

5. The word _____ comes from the Latin word linearis, which means created by lines.
   a. Linear0
   b. Thing
   c. Undefined
   d. Undefined

6. A _____ is an equation in which each term is either a constant or the product of a constant times the first power of a variable.
   a. Thing
   b. Linear equation0
   c. Undefined
   d. Undefined

7. A _____ is a negotiable instrument instructing a financial institution to pay a specific amount of a specific currency from a specific demand account held in the maker/depositor's name with that institution. Both the maker and payee may be natural persons or legal entities.
   a. Thing
   b. Check0
   c. Undefined
   d. Undefined

8. A _____ is a set of possible values that a variable can take on in order to satisfy a given set of conditions, which may include equations and inequalities.
   a. Solution set0
   b. Thing
   c. Undefined
   d. Undefined

9. _____ is a branch of mathematics concerning the study of structure, relation and quantity.
   a. Algebra0
   b. Concept
   c. Undefined
   d. Undefined

10. In mathematics, a _____ may be described informally as a number that can be given by an infinite decimal representation.

Chapter 3. LINEAR EQUATIONS AND INEQUALITIES

a. Real number0
b. Thing
c. Undefined
d. Undefined

11. In financial mathematics, the _____ volatility of an option contract is the volatility _____ by the market price of the option based on an option pricing model.
   a. Thing
   b. Implied0
   c. Undefined
   d. Undefined

12. Equivalence is the condition of being _____ or essentially equal.
   a. Thing
   b. Equivalent0
   c. Undefined
   d. Undefined

13. An _____ is a combination of numbers, operators, grouping symbols and/or free variables and bound variables arranged in a meaningful way which can be evaluated..
   a. Thing
   b. Expression0
   c. Undefined
   d. Undefined

14. A _____ is the result of the addition of a set of numbers. The numbers may be natural numbers, complex numbers, matrices, or still more complicated objects. An infinite _____ is a subtle procedure known as a series.
   a. Sum0
   b. Thing
   c. Undefined
   d. Undefined

15. In mathematics, the additive inverse, or _____ of a number n is the number that, when added to n, yields zero. The additive inverse of n is denoted −n. For example, 7 is −7, because 7 + (−7) = 0, and the additive inverse of −0.3 is 0.3, because −0.3 + 0.3 = 0.
   a. Thing
   b. Opposite0
   c. Undefined
   d. Undefined

16. In mathematics, the _____ of a number n is the number that, when added to n, yields zero. The _____ of n is denoted −n. For example, 7 is −7, because 7 + (−7) = 0, and the _____ of −0.3 is 0.3, because −0.3 + 0.3 = 0.
   a. Thing
   b. Additive inverse0
   c. Undefined
   d. Undefined

17. In mathematics, a _____ is a constant multiplicative factor of a certain object. The object can be such things as a variable, a vector, a function, etc. For example, the _____ of $9x^2$ is 9.
   a. Coefficient0
   b. Thing
   c. Undefined
   d. Undefined

18. In mathematics, the multiplicative inverse of a number x, denoted 1/x or x^{-1}, is the number which, when multiplied by x, yields 1. The multiplicative inverse of x is also called the _____ of x.
   a. Thing
   b. Reciprocal0
   c. Undefined
   d. Undefined

19. In mathematics, an _____ is a statement about the relative size or order of two objects.

Chapter 3. LINEAR EQUATIONS AND INEQUALITIES

a. Thing
b. Inequality0
c. Undefined
d. Undefined

20. In Euclidean geometry, a _____ is moving every point a constant distance in a specified direction.
a. Concept
b. Translation0
c. Undefined
d. Undefined

21. _____ over a given field is a polynomial with coefficients in that field.
a. Thing
b. Algebraic equation0
c. Undefined
d. Undefined

22. In mathematics, a _____ is the end result of a division problem. It can also be expressed as the number of times the divisor divides into the dividend.
a. Quotient0
b. Thing
c. Undefined
d. Undefined

23. In mathematics, a _____ is the result of multiplying, or an expression that identifies factors to be multiplied.
a. Product0
b. Thing
c. Undefined
d. Undefined

24. A _____ is a special kind of ratio, indicating a relationship between two measurements with different units, such as miles to gallons or cents to pounds.
a. Thing
b. Rate0
c. Undefined
d. Undefined

25. A _____ is a unit of length, usually used to measure distance, in a number of different systems, including Imperial units, United States customary units and Norwegian/Swedish mil. Its size can vary from system to system, but in each is between 1 and 10 kilometers. In contemporary English contexts _____ refers to either:
a. Thing
b. Mile0
c. Undefined
d. Undefined

26. In geometry, a _____ is defined as a quadrilateral where all four of its angles are right angles.
a. Rectangle0
b. Thing
c. Undefined
d. Undefined

27. A _____ of a number is the product of that number with any integer.
a. Thing
b. Multiple0
c. Undefined
d. Undefined

28. An _____ is an equality that remains true regardless of the values of any variables that appear within it, to distinguish it from an equality which is true under more particular conditions.
a. Thing
b. Identity0
c. Undefined
d. Undefined

29. _____, either of the curved-bracket punctuation marks that together make a set of _____

Chapter 3. LINEAR EQUATIONS AND INEQUALITIES

    a. Thing
    b. Parentheses0
    c. Undefined
    d. Undefined

30. In mathematics and the mathematical sciences, a _____ is a fixed, but possibly unspecified, value. This is in contrast to a variable, which is not fixed.
    a. Thing
    b. Constant0
    c. Undefined
    d. Undefined

31. _____ is a fixed, but possibly unspecified, value. This is in contrast to a variable, which is not fixed.
    a. Constant term0
    b. Thing
    c. Undefined
    d. Undefined

32. In logic, a _____ consists of a logical incompatibility between two or more propositions.
    a. Contradictions0
    b. Thing
    c. Undefined
    d. Undefined

33. The material _____, also known as the material implication or truth functional _____, expresses a property of certain conditionals in logic.
    a. Thing
    b. Conditional0
    c. Undefined
    d. Undefined

34. In mathematics, _____ expressions is used to reduce the expression into the lowest possible term.
    a. Thing
    b. Simplifying0
    c. Undefined
    d. Undefined

35. _____ forms part of thinking. Considered the most complex of all intellectual functions, _____ has been defined as higher-order cognitive process that requires the modulation and control of more routine or fundamental skills.
    a. Problem solving0
    b. Thing
    c. Undefined
    d. Undefined

36. The plus and _____ signs are mathematical symbols used to represent the notions of positive and negative as well as the operations of addition and subtraction.
    a. Thing
    b. Minus0
    c. Undefined
    d. Undefined

37. A _____ is a quantity that denotes the proportional amount or magnitude of one quantity relative to another.
    a. Thing
    b. Ratio0
    c. Undefined
    d. Undefined

38. The _____, the average in everyday English, which is also called the arithmetic _____ (and is distinguished from the geometric _____ or harmonic _____). The average is also called the sample _____. The expected value of a random variable, which is also called the population _____.
    a. Thing
    b. Mean0
    c. Undefined
    d. Undefined

39. _____ means in succession or back-to-back

Chapter 3. LINEAR EQUATIONS AND INEQUALITIES

    a. Thing
    c. Undefined
    b. Consecutive0
    d. Undefined

40. _____ (Groups, Algorithms and Programming) is a computer algebra system for computational discrete algebra with particular emphasis on, but not restricted to, computational group theory.
    a. Thing
    b. Gap0
    c. Undefined
    d. Undefined

41. The _____ are the only integral domain whose positive elements are well-ordered, and in which order is preserved by addition. Like the natural numbers, the _____ form a countably infinite set. The set of all _____ is usually denoted in mathematics by a boldface Z .
    a. Thing
    b. Integers0
    c. Undefined
    d. Undefined

42. The _____ of measurement are a globally standardized and modernized form of the metric system.
    a. Units0
    b. Thing
    c. Undefined
    d. Undefined

43. In _____ algebra, a *-ring is an associative ring with an antilinear, antiautomorphism * : A ¨ A which is an involution.
    a. Star0
    b. Thing
    c. Undefined
    d. Undefined

44. _____ is a business term for the amount of money that a company receives from its activities in a given period, mostly from sales of products and/or services to customers
    a. Thing
    b. Revenue0
    c. Undefined
    d. Undefined

45. In mathematics, an _____, mean, or central tendency of a data set refers to a measure of the "middle" or "expected" value of the data set.
    a. Concept
    b. Average0
    c. Undefined
    d. Undefined

46. In mathematics, a _____ of a positive integer n is a way of writing n as a sum of positive integers.
    a. Thing
    b. Composition0
    c. Undefined
    d. Undefined

47. In geometry, a _____ is any five-sided polygon.
    a. Pentagon0
    b. Thing
    c. Undefined
    d. Undefined

48. _____ is the distance around a given two-dimensional object. As a general rule, the _____ of a polygon can always be calculated by adding all the length of the sides together. So, the formula for triangles is P = a + b + c, where a, b and c stand for each side of it. For quadrilaterals the equation is P = a + b + c + d. For equilateral polygons, P = na, where n is the number of sides and a is the side length.

Chapter 3. LINEAR EQUATIONS AND INEQUALITIES

    a. Perimeter0
    c. Undefined
    b. Thing
    d. Undefined

49. In geometry a _____ is a plane figure that is bounded by a closed path or circuit, composed of a finite number of sequential line segments.
    a. Polygon0
    c. Undefined
    b. Thing
    d. Undefined

50. A _____ is a landform that extends above the surrounding terrain in a limited area. A _____ is generally steeper than a hill, but there is no universally accepted standard definition for the height of a _____ or a hill although a _____ usually has an identifiable summit.
    a. Thing
    c. Undefined
    b. Mountain0
    d. Undefined

51. The payment of _____ as remuneration for services rendered or products sold is a common way to reward sales people.
    a. Commission0
    c. Undefined
    b. Thing
    d. Undefined

52. _____ is a way of expressing a number as a fraction of 100 per cent meaning "per hundred".
    a. Thing
    c. Undefined
    b. Percent0
    d. Undefined

53. _____ is the fee paid on borrowed money.
    a. Interest0
    c. Undefined
    b. Thing
    d. Undefined

54. A _____ is a consumption tax charged at the point of purchase for certain goods and services.
    a. Sales tax0
    c. Undefined
    b. Thing
    d. Undefined

55. A _____ is the part of a fraction that tells how many equal parts make up a whole, and which is used in the name of the fraction: "halves", "thirds", "fourths" or "quarters", "fifths" and so on.
    a. Denominator0
    c. Undefined
    b. Concept
    d. Undefined

56. _____ is the largest positive integer that divides both numbers without remainder.
    a. Thing
    c. Undefined
    b. Common Factor0
    d. Undefined

57. In mathematics, factorization (British English: factorisation) or factoring is the decomposition of an object (for example, a number, a polynomial, or a matrix) into a product of other objects, or _____, which when multiplied together give the original.
    a. Factors0
    c. Undefined
    b. Thing
    d. Undefined

Chapter 3. LINEAR EQUATIONS AND INEQUALITIES

58. In mathematics, and in particular in abstract algebra, the _____ is a property of binary operations that generalises the distributive law from elementary algebra.
   a. Distributive property0
   b. Thing
   c. Undefined
   d. Undefined

59. Regrouping is the act of putting ones into groups of 10. For example, the 1 on the far right of 131 would be denoted _____ if the digit of the number being subtracted is larger than 1, such as 131-99.
   a. By 100
   b. Thing
   c. Undefined
   d. Undefined

60. The decimal separator is a symbol used to mark the boundary between the integral and the fractional parts of a decimal numeral. Terms implying the symbol used are _____ and decimal comma.
   a. Decimal point0
   b. Concept
   c. Undefined
   d. Undefined

61. A _____ is a type of debt. All material things can be lent but this article focuses exclusively on monetary loans. Like all debt instruments, a _____ entails the redistribution of financial assets over time, between the lender and the borrower.
   a. Loan0
   b. Thing
   c. Undefined
   d. Undefined

62. _____ or investing is a term with several closely-related meanings in business management, finance and economics, related to saving or deferring consumption.
   a. Thing
   b. Investment0
   c. Undefined
   d. Undefined

63. In geometry, the _____ of an object is a point in some sense in the middle of the object.
   a. Center0
   b. Thing
   c. Undefined
   d. Undefined

64. _____, from Latin meaning "to make progress", is defined in two different ways. Pure economic _____ is the increase in wealth that an investor has from making an investment, taking into consideration all costs associated with that investment including the opportunity cost of capital.
   a. Thing
   b. Profit0
   c. Undefined
   d. Undefined

65. In finance and economics, _____ is the process of finding the present value of an amount of cash at some future date, and along with compounding cash forms the basis of time value of money calculations.
   a. Discount0
   b. Thing
   c. Undefined
   d. Undefined

66. _____ is a form of periodic payment from an employer to an employee, which is specified in an employment contract.
   a. Gross pay0
   b. Thing
   c. Undefined
   d. Undefined

Chapter 3. LINEAR EQUATIONS AND INEQUALITIES

67. A _____ is a form of periodic payment from an employer to an employee, which is specified in an employment contract.
   a. Salary0
   b. Thing
   c. Undefined
   d. Undefined

68. The _____ (symbol _____) and the millibar (symbol mbar, also mb) are units of pressure.
   a. Bar0
   b. Thing
   c. Undefined
   d. Undefined

69. An _____ is the fee paid on borrow money.
   a. Concept
   b. Interest rate0
   c. Undefined
   d. Undefined

70. _____ is the transport of people on a trip/journey or the process or time involved in a person or object moving from one location to another.
   a. Thing
   b. Travel0
   c. Undefined
   d. Undefined

71. A _____ is a numeral used to indicate a count. The most common use of the word today is to name the part of a fraction that tells the number or count of equal parts.
   a. Thing
   b. Numerator0
   c. Undefined
   d. Undefined

72. In mathematics, a _____ of an integer n, also called a factor of n, is an integer which evenly divides n without leaving a remainder.
   a. Divisor0
   b. Thing
   c. Undefined
   d. Undefined

73. _____ is a temperature scale named after the German physicist Daniel Gabriel _____, who proposed it in 1724.
   a. Thing
   b. Fahrenheit0
   c. Undefined
   d. Undefined

74. _____ is, or relates to, the _____ temperature scale .
   a. Thing
   b. Celsius0
   c. Undefined
   d. Undefined

75. In mathematics, there are several meanings of _____ depending on the subject.
   a. Thing
   b. Degree0
   c. Undefined
   d. Undefined

76. _____ is a physical property of a system that underlies the common notions of hot and cold; something that is hotter has the greater _____.
   a. Thing
   b. Temperature0
   c. Undefined
   d. Undefined

Chapter 3. LINEAR EQUATIONS AND INEQUALITIES

77. A pair of angles are _____ if the sum of their angles is 90°.
    a. Concept
    b. Complementary0
    c. Undefined
    d. Undefined

78. A _____ is one of the basic shapes of geometry: a polygon with three vertices and three sides which are straight line segments.
    a. Triangle0
    b. Thing
    c. Undefined
    d. Undefined

79. A _____ is a function that assigns a number to subsets of a given set.
    a. Measure0
    b. Thing
    c. Undefined
    d. Undefined

80. The _____ is the distance around a closed curve. _____ is a kind of perimeter.
    a. Circumference0
    b. Thing
    c. Undefined
    d. Undefined

81. In classical geometry, a _____ of a circle or sphere is any line segment from its center to its boundary. By extension, the _____ of a circle or sphere is the length of any such segment. The _____ is half the diameter. In science and engineering the term _____ of curvature is commonly used as a synonym for _____.
    a. Thing
    b. Radius0
    c. Undefined
    d. Undefined

82. In arithmetic and algebra, when a number or expression is both preceded and followed by a binary operation, an _____ is required for which operation should be applied first.
    a. Order of operations0
    b. Thing
    c. Undefined
    d. Undefined

83. In plane geometry, a _____ is a polygon with four equal sides, four right angles, and parallel opposite sides. In algebra, the _____ of a number is that number multiplied by itself.
    a. Square0
    b. Thing
    c. Undefined
    d. Undefined

84. An n-sided _____ is a polyhedron formed by connecting an n-sided polygonal base and a point, called the apex, by n triangular faces. In other words, it is a conic solid with polygonal base.
    a. Thing
    b. Pyramid0
    c. Undefined
    d. Undefined

85. In Euclidean geometry, a _____ is the set of all points in a plane at a fixed distance, called the radius, from a given point, the center.
    a. Circle0
    b. Thing
    c. Undefined
    d. Undefined

86. The _____ of a solid object is the three-dimensional concept of how much space it occupies, often quantified numerically.

a. Thing
b. Volume0
c. Undefined
d. Undefined

87. In mathematics, _____ geometry was the traditional name for the geometry of three-dimensional Euclidean space — for practical purposes the kind of space we live in.
   a. Solid0
   b. Thing
   c. Undefined
   d. Undefined

88. In mathematics, a _____ is a quadric surface, with the following equation in Cartesian coordinates: $(x/_a)^2 + (y/_b)^2 = 1$.
   a. Thing
   b. Cylinder0
   c. Undefined
   d. Undefined

89. A _____ is a quadrilateral, which is defined as a shape with four sides, which has a pair of parallel sides.
   a. Trapezoid0
   b. Thing
   c. Undefined
   d. Undefined

90. In mathematics, a _____ is the set of all points in three-dimensional space (R^3) which are at distance r from a fixed point of that space, where r is a positive real number called the radius of the _____. The fixed point is called the center or centre, and is not part of the _____ itself.
   a. Thing
   b. Sphere0
   c. Undefined
   d. Undefined

91. A pair of angles is _____ if their respective measures sum to 180 degrees.
   a. Concept
   b. Supplementary0
   c. Undefined
   d. Undefined

92. A pair of angles are said to be _____ if they share the same vertex and are bounded by the same pair of lines but are opposite to each other. They are also congruent.
   a. Vertical angles0
   b. Thing
   c. Undefined
   d. Undefined

93. A _____ fraction is a fraction in which the absolute value of the numerator is less than the denominator--hence, the absolute value of the fraction is less than 1.
   a. Thing
   b. Proper0
   c. Undefined
   d. Undefined

94. In combinatorial mathematics, a _____ is an un-ordered collection of unique elements.
   a. Combination0
   b. Concept
   c. Undefined
   d. Undefined

95. In mathematics, a _____ is a condition that a solution to an optimization problem must satisfy in order to be acceptable.
   a. Constraint0
   b. Thing
   c. Undefined
   d. Undefined

Chapter 3. LINEAR EQUATIONS AND INEQUALITIES

96. In chemistry, a _____ is substance made by combining two or more different materials in such a way that no chemical reaction occurs.
- a. Mixture0
- b. Thing
- c. Undefined
- d. Undefined

97. _____ is a special mathematical relationship between two quantities. Two quantities are called proportional if they vary in such a way that one of the quantities is a constant multiple of the other, or equivalently if they have a constant ratio.
- a. Thing
- b. Proportionality0
- c. Undefined
- d. Undefined

98. _____ is a kind of property which exists as magnitude or multitude. It is among the basic classes of things along with quality, substance, change, and relation.
- a. Amount0
- b. Thing
- c. Undefined
- d. Undefined

99. In mathematics, a matrix can be thought of as each row or _____ being a vector. Hence, a space formed by row vectors or _____ vectors are said to be a row space or a _____ space.
- a. Column0
- b. Concept
- c. Undefined
- d. Undefined

100. _____ is a binary operation on two vectors in a three-dimensional Euclidean space that results in another vector which is perpedicular to the two input vectors.
- a. Thing
- b. Cross product0
- c. Undefined
- d. Undefined

101. _____ traditionally refers to the statistical process of determining comparable scores on different forms of an exam
- a. Thing
- b. Equating0
- c. Undefined
- d. Undefined

102. _____ (or proportionality) are two quantities that vary in such a way that one of the quatities is a constant multiple of the other, or equivalently if they have a constant ratio.
- a. Thing
- b. Proportions0
- c. Undefined
- d. Undefined

103. In mathematics, two quantities are called _____ if they vary in such a way that one of the quantities is a constant multiple of the other, or equivalently if they have a constant ratio.
- a. Thing
- b. Proportional0
- c. Undefined
- d. Undefined

104. _____ is the estimation of a physical quantity such as distance, energy, temperature, or time.
- a. Measurement0
- b. Thing
- c. Undefined
- d. Undefined

Chapter 3. LINEAR EQUATIONS AND INEQUALITIES

105. A _____ are accounts maintained by commercial banks, savings and loan associations, credit unions, and mutual savings banks that pay interest but can not be used directly as money by, for example, writing a cheque.
   a. Savings account0
   b. Thing
   c. Undefined
   d. Undefined

106. In set theory and other branches of mathematics, the _____ of a collection of sets is the set that contains everything that belongs to any of the sets, but nothing else.
   a. Thing
   b. Union0
   c. Undefined
   d. Undefined

107. In mathematics, a _____ is a two-dimensional manifold or surface that is perfectly flat.
   a. Plane0
   b. Thing
   c. Undefined
   d. Undefined

108. In botany, _____ are above-ground plant organs specialized for photosynthesis. Their characteristics are typically analyzed by using Fiobonacci's sequences.
   a. Thing
   b. Leaves0
   c. Undefined
   d. Undefined

109. _____ is a subset of a population.
   a. Thing
   b. Sample0
   c. Undefined
   d. Undefined

110. _____ is electromagnetic radiation with a wavelength that is visible to the eye (visible _____) or, in a technical or scientific context, electromagnetic radiation of any wavelength.
   a. Light0
   b. Thing
   c. Undefined
   d. Undefined

111. Mathematical _____ is used to represent ideas.
   a. Thing
   b. Notation0
   c. Undefined
   d. Undefined

112. A _____ is a one-dimensional picture in which the integers are shown as specially-marked points evenly spaced on a line.
   a. Number line0
   b. Thing
   c. Undefined
   d. Undefined

113. In elementary algebra, an _____ is a set that contains every real number between two indicated numbers and may contain the two numbers themselves.
   a. Thing
   b. Interval0
   c. Undefined
   d. Undefined

114. _____ is the state of being greater than any finite real or natural number, however large.
   a. Infinite0
   b. Thing
   c. Undefined
   d. Undefined

Chapter 3. LINEAR EQUATIONS AND INEQUALITIES

115. In mathematics, _____ are used in a variety of notations, including standard notations for intervals, commutators, the Lie bracket, and the Iverson bracket.
   a. Thing
   b. Square Brackets0
   c. Undefined
   d. Undefined

116. In mathematics, an inequality is a statement about the relative size or order of two objects. For example 14 > 10, or 14 is _____ 10.
   a. Thing
   b. Greater than0
   c. Undefined
   d. Undefined

117. _____ interest refers to the fact that whenever interest is calculated, it is based not only on the original principal, but also on any unpaid interest that has been added to the principal.
   a. Thing
   b. Compound0
   c. Undefined
   d. Undefined

118. _____ is the notation in which permitted values for a variable are expressed as ranging over a certain interval; "5 < x < 9" is an example of the application of _____.
   a. Thing
   b. Interval notation0
   c. Undefined
   d. Undefined

119. _____ is the state of being greater than any finite number, however large.
   a. Infinity0
   b. Thing
   c. Undefined
   d. Undefined

120. In geometry, an _____ is a point at which a line segment or ray terminates.
   a. Thing
   b. Endpoint0
   c. Undefined
   d. Undefined

121. Acid _____ ratio measures the ability of a company to use its near cash or quick assets to immediately extinguish its current liabilities.
   a. Test0
   b. Thing
   c. Undefined
   d. Undefined

122. _____ is a term applied when talking about the movement of air from one place to the next.
   a. Thing
   b. Wind speed0
   c. Undefined
   d. Undefined

123. An _____ is a collection of two not necessarily distinct objects, one of which is distinguished as the first coordinate and the other as the second coordinate.
   a. Ordered pair0
   b. Thing
   c. Undefined
   d. Undefined

124. A _____ is a set of numbers that designate location in a given reference system, such as x,y in a planar _____ system or an x,y,z in a three-dimensional _____ system.

Chapter 3. LINEAR EQUATIONS AND INEQUALITIES

    a. Coordinate0
    c. Undefined
    b. Thing
    d. Undefined

125. In mathematics and its applications, a _____ is a system for assigning an n-tuple of numbers or scalars to each point in an n-dimensional space.
    a. Concept
    b. Coordinate system0
    c. Undefined
    d. Undefined

126. In mathematics, the conjugate _____ or adjoint matrix of an m-by-n matrix A with complex entries is the n-by-m matrix A* obtained from A by taking the transpose and then taking the complex conjugate of each entry.
    a. Thing
    b. Pairs0
    c. Undefined
    d. Undefined

127. In Euclidean geometry, a uniform _____ is a linear transformation that enlargers or diminishes objects, and whose _____ factor is the same in all directions. This is also called homothethy.
    a. Scale0
    b. Thing
    c. Undefined
    d. Undefined

128. In mathematics, the _____ of a function is the set of all "output" values produced by that function. Given a function $f : A \rightarrow B$, the _____ of f, is defined to be the set $\{x \in B : x = f(a) \text{ for some } a \in A\}$.
    a. Range0
    b. Thing
    c. Undefined
    d. Undefined

129. In geographic information systems, a _____ comprises an entity with a geographic location, typically determined by points, arcs, or polygons. Carriageways and cadastres exemplify _____ data.
    a. Thing
    b. Feature0
    c. Undefined
    d. Undefined

130. In topology and related areas of mathematics a _____ or Moore-Smith sequence is a generalization of a sequence, intended to unify the various notions of limit and generalize them to arbitrary topological spaces.
    a. Net0
    b. Thing
    c. Undefined
    d. Undefined

131. _____ is a three-dimensional geometric shape formed by straight lines through a fixed point vertex to the points of a fixed curve directrix.
    a. Thing
    b. Right circular cone0
    c. Undefined
    d. Undefined

132. A _____ is a three-dimensional geometric shape formed by straight lines through a fixed point (vertex) to the points of a fixed curve (directrix)
    a. Cone0
    b. Concept
    c. Undefined
    d. Undefined

133. A _____ is a four-sided plane figure that has two sets of opposite parallel sides.

Chapter 3. LINEAR EQUATIONS AND INEQUALITIES

a. Concept
b. Parallelogram0
c. Undefined
d. Undefined

134. U.S. liquid _____ is legally defined as 231 cubic inches, and is equal to 3.785411784 litres or abotu 0.13368 cubic feet. This is the most common definition of a _____. The U.S. fluid ounce is defined as 1/128 of a U.S. _____.
a. Gallon0
b. Thing
c. Undefined
d. Undefined

135. _____ are a measure of time.
a. Minutes0
b. Thing
c. Undefined
d. Undefined

136. A _____ consists of one quarter of the coordinate plane.
a. Thing
b. Quadrant0
c. Undefined
d. Undefined

137. An _____ is a straight line around which a geometric figure can be rotated.
a. Thing
b. Axis0
c. Undefined
d. Undefined

138. _____ is a relation in Euclidean geometry among the three sides of a right triangle.
a. Thing
b. Pythagorean Theorem0
c. Undefined
d. Undefined

139. In mathematics, a _____ is a statement that can be proved on the basis of explicitly stated or previously agreed assumptions.
a. Thing
b. Theorem0
c. Undefined
d. Undefined

Chapter 4. POLYNOMIALS AND PROPERTIES OF EXPONENTS

1. In mathematics, _____ is an elementary arithmetic operation. When one of the numbers is a whole number, _____ is the repeated sum of the other number.
   a. Multiplication0
   b. Thing
   c. Undefined
   d. Undefined

2. Mathematical _____ is used to represent ideas.
   a. Notation0
   b. Thing
   c. Undefined
   d. Undefined

3. In mathematics, _____ growth occurs when the growth rate of a function is always proportional to the function's current size.
   a. Exponential0
   b. Thing
   c. Undefined
   d. Undefined

4. _____ is a notation for writing numbers that is often used by scientists and mathematicians to make it easier to write large and small numbers.
   a. Thing
   b. Scientific notation0
   c. Undefined
   d. Undefined

5. In mathematics, a _____ may be described informally as a number that can be given by an infinite decimal representation.
   a. Real number0
   b. Thing
   c. Undefined
   d. Undefined

6. A _____ is a number that is less than zero.
   a. Negative number0
   b. Thing
   c. Undefined
   d. Undefined

7. _____ is a mathematical operation, written a^n, involving two numbers, the base a and the exponent n.
   a. Thing
   b. Exponentiating0
   c. Undefined
   d. Undefined

8. _____ is a mathematical operation, written a^n, involving two numbers, the base a and the exponent n.
   a. Exponentiation0
   b. Thing
   c. Undefined
   d. Undefined

9. An _____ is a combination of numbers, operators, grouping symbols and/or free variables and bound variables arranged in a meaningful way which can be evaluated..
   a. Expression0
   b. Thing
   c. Undefined
   d. Undefined

10. In financial mathematics, the _____ volatility of an option contract is the volatility _____ by the market price of the option based on an option pricing model.
    a. Thing
    b. Implied0
    c. Undefined
    d. Undefined

11. In mathematics, _____ expressions is used to reduce the expression into the lowest possible term.

Chapter 4. POLYNOMIALS AND PROPERTIES OF EXPONENTS

a. Thing
b. Simplifying0
c. Undefined
d. Undefined

12. In mathematics, the additive inverse, or _____ of a number n is the number that, when added to n, yields zero. The additive inverse of n is denoted −n. For example, 7 is −7, because 7 + (−7) = 0, and the additive inverse of −0.3 is 0.3, because −0.3 + 0.3 = 0.
a. Thing
b. Opposite0
c. Undefined
d. Undefined

13. _____, either of the curved-bracket punctuation marks that together make a set of _____
a. Thing
b. Parentheses0
c. Undefined
d. Undefined

14. In mathematics, the _____ of a number n is the number that, when added to n, yields zero. The _____ of n is denoted −n. For example, 7 is −7, because 7 + (−7) = 0, and the _____ of −0.3 is 0.3, because −0.3 + 0.3 = 0.
a. Thing
b. Additive inverse0
c. Undefined
d. Undefined

15. A _____ is a symbolic representation denoting a quantity or expression. It often represents an "unknown" quantity that has the potential to change.
a. Variable0
b. Thing
c. Undefined
d. Undefined

16. In arithmetic and algebra, when a number or expression is both preceded and followed by a binary operation, an _____ is required for which operation should be applied first.
a. Thing
b. Order of operations0
c. Undefined
d. Undefined

17. In mathematics, a _____ is an expression that is constructed from one or more variables and constants, using only the operations of addition, subtraction, multiplication, and constant positive whole number exponents. is a _____. Note in particular that division by an expression containing a variable is not in general allowed in polynomials. [1]
a. Thing
b. Polynomial0
c. Undefined
d. Undefined

18. In mathematics and the mathematical sciences, a _____ is a fixed, but possibly unspecified, value. This is in contrast to a variable, which is not fixed.
a. Thing
b. Constant0
c. Undefined
d. Undefined

19. In plane geometry, a _____ is a polygon with four equal sides, four right angles, and parallel opposite sides. In algebra, the _____ of a number is that number multiplied by itself.
a. Thing
b. Square0
c. Undefined
d. Undefined

20. A _____ is a numeral used to indicate a count. The most common use of the word today is to name the part of a fraction that tells the number or count of equal parts.

Chapter 4. POLYNOMIALS AND PROPERTIES OF EXPONENTS

a. Numerator0
b. Thing
c. Undefined
d. Undefined

21. A _____ is the part of a fraction that tells how many equal parts make up a whole, and which is used in the name of the fraction: "halves", "thirds", "fourths" or "quarters", "fifths" and so on.
    a. Concept
    b. Denominator0
    c. Undefined
    d. Undefined

22. The _____ are the only integral domain whose positive elements are well-ordered, and in which order is preserved by addition. Like the natural numbers, the _____ form a countably infinite set. The set of all _____ is usually denoted in mathematics by a boldface Z .
    a. Integers0
    b. Thing
    c. Undefined
    d. Undefined

23. Equivalence is the condition of being _____ or essentially equal.
    a. Equivalent0
    b. Thing
    c. Undefined
    d. Undefined

24. A _____ fraction is a fraction in which the absolute value of the numerator is less than the denominator--hence, the absolute value of the fraction is less than 1.
    a. Thing
    b. Proper0
    c. Undefined
    d. Undefined

25. In mathematics, a _____ is a constant multiplicative factor of a certain object. The object can be such things as a variable, a vector, a function, etc. For example, the _____ of $9x^2$ is 9.
    a. Thing
    b. Coefficient0
    c. Undefined
    d. Undefined

26. In mathematics, factorization (British English: factorisation) or factoring is the decomposition of an object (for example, a number, a polynomial, or a matrix) into a product of other objects, or _____, which when multiplied together give the original.
    a. Factors0
    b. Thing
    c. Undefined
    d. Undefined

27. A _____ is a special kind of ratio, indicating a relationship between two measurements with different units, such as miles to gallons or cents to pounds.
    a. Thing
    b. Rate0
    c. Undefined
    d. Undefined

28. A _____ is a type of debt. All material things can be lent but this article focuses exclusively on monetary loans. Like all debt instruments, a _____ entails the redistribution of financial assets over time, between the lender and the borrower.
    a. Loan0
    b. Thing
    c. Undefined
    d. Undefined

Chapter 4. POLYNOMIALS AND PROPERTIES OF EXPONENTS

29. _____ is a kind of property which exists as magnitude or multitude. It is among the basic classes of things along with quality, substance, change, and relation.
   a. Amount0
   b. Thing
   c. Undefined
   d. Undefined

30. _____ is the fee paid on borrowed money.
   a. Interest0
   b. Thing
   c. Undefined
   d. Undefined

31. An _____ is the fee paid on borrow money.
   a. Interest rate0
   b. Concept
   c. Undefined
   d. Undefined

32. _____ or investing is a term with several closely-related meanings in business management, finance and economics, related to saving or deferring consumption.
   a. Thing
   b. Investment0
   c. Undefined
   d. Undefined

33. _____ interest refers to the fact that whenever interest is calculated, it is based not only on the original principal, but also on any unpaid interest that has been added to the principal.
   a. Thing
   b. Compound0
   c. Undefined
   d. Undefined

34. _____ refers to the fact that whenever interest is calculated, it is based not only on the original principal, but also on any unpaid interest that has been added to the principal. The more frequently interest is compounded, the faster the balance grows.
   a. Compound interest0
   b. Concept
   c. Undefined
   d. Undefined

35. In business, particularly accounting, a _____ is the time intervals that the accounts, statement, payments, or other calculations cover.
   a. Period0
   b. Thing
   c. Undefined
   d. Undefined

36. _____ is the process of reducing the number of significant digits in a number.
   a. Rounding0
   b. Concept
   c. Undefined
   d. Undefined

37. Initial objects are also called _____, and terminal objects are also called final.
   a. Coterminal0
   b. Thing
   c. Undefined
   d. Undefined

Chapter 4. POLYNOMIALS AND PROPERTIES OF EXPONENTS

38. In geometry, a _____ (Greek words diairo = divide and metro = measure) of a circle is any straight line segment that passes through the centre and whose endpoints are on the circular boundary, or, in more modern usage, the length of such a line segment. When using the word in the more modern sense, one speaks of the _____ rather than a _____, because all diameters of a circle have the same length. This length is twice the radius. The _____ of a circle is also the longest chord that the circle has.
   a. Diameter0
   b. Thing
   c. Undefined
   d. Undefined

39. The _____ of a solid object is the three-dimensional concept of how much space it occupies, often quantified numerically.
   a. Volume0
   b. Thing
   c. Undefined
   d. Undefined

40. In mathematics, a _____ is the set of all points in three-dimensional space (R^3) which are at distance r from a fixed point of that space, where r is a positive real number called the radius of the _____. The fixed point is called the center or centre, and is not part of the _____ itself.
   a. Thing
   b. Sphere0
   c. Undefined
   d. Undefined

41. Compass and straightedge or ruler-and-compass _____ is the _____ of lengths or angles using only an idealized ruler and compass.
   a. Construction0
   b. Thing
   c. Undefined
   d. Undefined

42. A _____ is a three-dimensional solid object bounded by six square faces, facets, or sides, with three meeting at each vertex.
   a. Cube0
   b. Thing
   c. Undefined
   d. Undefined

43. _____ has many meanings, most of which simply .
   a. Power0
   b. Thing
   c. Undefined
   d. Undefined

44. _____ is a method for differentiating expressions involving exponentiation the power operation.
   a. Thing
   b. Power rule0
   c. Undefined
   d. Undefined

45. In mathematics, a _____ is the result of multiplying, or an expression that identifies factors to be multiplied.
   a. Product0
   b. Thing
   c. Undefined
   d. Undefined

46. In mathematics, a _____ is the end result of a division problem. It can also be expressed as the number of times the divisor divides into the dividend.
   a. Thing
   b. Quotient0
   c. Undefined
   d. Undefined

Chapter 4. POLYNOMIALS AND PROPERTIES OF EXPONENTS

47. In Euclidean geometry, a _____ is moving every point a constant distance in a specified direction.
    a. Concept
    b. Translation0
    c. Undefined
    d. Undefined

48. In mathematics, an inequality is a statement about the relative size or order of two objects. For example 14 > 10, or 14 is _____ 10.
    a. Greater than0
    b. Thing
    c. Undefined
    d. Undefined

49. In mathematics, the multiplicative inverse of a number x, denoted 1/x or x^{-1}, is the number which, when multiplied by x, yields 1. The multiplicative inverse of x is also called the _____ of x.
    a. Thing
    b. Reciprocal0
    c. Undefined
    d. Undefined

50. A _____ is a deliberate process for transforming one or more inputs into one or more results.
    a. Calculation0
    b. Thing
    c. Undefined
    d. Undefined

51. A _____ signifies a point or points of probability on a subject e.g., the _____ of creativity, which allows for the formation of rule or norm or law by interpretation of the phenomena events that can be created.
    a. Principle0
    b. Thing
    c. Undefined
    d. Undefined

52. The _____ of a mathematical object is its size: a property by which it can be larger or smaller than other objects of the same kind; in technical terms, an ordering of the class of objects to which it belongs.
    a. Magnitude0
    b. Thing
    c. Undefined
    d. Undefined

53. The decimal separator is a symbol used to mark the boundary between the integral and the fractional parts of a decimal numeral. Terms implying the symbol used are _____ and decimal comma.
    a. Concept
    b. Decimal point0
    c. Undefined
    d. Undefined

54. _____ is the property of a physical object that quantifies the amount of matter and energy it is equivalent to.
    a. Thing
    b. Mass0
    c. Undefined
    d. Undefined

55. In mathematics, _____ is a property that a binary operation can have. Within an expression containing two or more of the same associative operators in a row, the order of operations does not matter as long as the sequence of the operands is not changed.
    a. Associativity0
    b. Thing
    c. Undefined
    d. Undefined

56. _____ is the transport of people on a trip/journey or the process or time involved in a person or object moving from one location to another.

a. Travel0
b. Thing
c. Undefined
d. Undefined

57. A _____ is a unit of length, usually used to measure distance, in a number of different systems, including Imperial units, United States customary units and Norwegian/Swedish mil. Its size can vary from system to system, but in each is between 1 and 10 kilometers. In contemporary English contexts _____ refers to either:
   a. Mile0
   b. Thing
   c. Undefined
   d. Undefined

58. _____ is a business term for the amount of money that a company receives from its activities in a given period, mostly from sales of products and/or services to customers
   a. Thing
   b. Revenue0
   c. Undefined
   d. Undefined

59. The _____, the average in everyday English, which is also called the arithmetic _____ (and is distinguished from the geometric _____ or harmonic _____). The average is also called the sample _____. The expected value of a random variable, which is also called the population _____.
   a. Thing
   b. Mean0
   c. Undefined
   d. Undefined

60. _____ is a unit of length in the metric system, equal to one billionth of a metre, which is the current SI base unit of length.
   a. Nanometer0
   b. Thing
   c. Undefined
   d. Undefined

61. _____ is a state located in the southern and southwestern regions of the United States of America.
   a. Thing
   b. Texas0
   c. Undefined
   d. Undefined

62. A _____ is the result of the addition of a set of numbers. The numbers may be natural numbers, complex numbers, matrices, or still more complicated objects. An infinite _____ is a subtle procedure known as a series.
   a. Thing
   b. Sum0
   c. Undefined
   d. Undefined

63. In mathematics, an _____, mean, or central tendency of a data set refers to a measure of the "middle" or "expected" value of the data set.
   a. Average0
   b. Concept
   c. Undefined
   d. Undefined

64. In topology and related areas of mathematics a _____ or Moore-Smith sequence is a generalization of a sequence, intended to unify the various notions of limit and generalize them to arbitrary topological spaces.
   a. Net0
   b. Thing
   c. Undefined
   d. Undefined

65. A _____ is a compensation which workers receive in exchange for their labor.

Chapter 4. POLYNOMIALS AND PROPERTIES OF EXPONENTS

a. Wage0
b. Thing
c. Undefined
d. Undefined

66. In physics, _____ is an influence that may cause an object to accelerate. It may be experienced as a lift, a push, or a pull. The actual acceleration of the body is determined by the vector sum of all forces acting on it, known as net _____ or resultant _____.
   a. Thing
   b. Force0
   c. Undefined
   d. Undefined

67. In sociology and biology a _____ is the collection of people or organisms of a particular species living in a given geographic area or space, usually measured by a census.
   a. Thing
   b. Population0
   c. Undefined
   d. Undefined

68. _____ is the chance that something is likely to happen or be the case.
   a. Probability0
   b. Thing
   c. Undefined
   d. Undefined

69. In mathematics, a _____ is a particular kind of polynomial, having just one term.
   a. Monomial0
   b. Thing
   c. Undefined
   d. Undefined

70. In elementary algebra, a _____ is a polynomial with two terms: the sum of two monomials. It is the simplest kind of polynomial except for a monomial.
   a. Binomial0
   b. Thing
   c. Undefined
   d. Undefined

71. The _____ integers are all the integers from zero on upwards.
   a. Nonnegative0
   b. Thing
   c. Undefined
   d. Undefined

72. In mathematics, there are several meanings of _____ depending on the subject.
   a. Thing
   b. Degree0
   c. Undefined
   d. Undefined

73. The _____ is the maximum of the degrees of all terms in the polynomial.
   a. Thing
   b. Degree of a polynomial0
   c. Undefined
   d. Undefined

74. The _____ is the sum of the exponents of the variables in the term.
   a. Thing
   b. Degree of a term0
   c. Undefined
   d. Undefined

75. In mathematics, and in particular in abstract algebra, the _____ is a property of binary operations that generalises the distributive law from elementary algebra.

Chapter 4. POLYNOMIALS AND PROPERTIES OF EXPONENTS

    a. Distributive property0
    b. Thing
    c. Undefined
    d. Undefined

76. In mathematics, a matrix can be thought of as each row or _____ being a vector. Hence, a space formed by row vectors or _____ vectors are said to be a row space or a _____ space.
    a. Column0
    b. Concept
    c. Undefined
    d. Undefined

77. _____ element of an element x with respect to a binary operation * with identity element e is an element y such that x * y = y * x = e. In particular,
    a. Thing
    b. Inverse0
    c. Undefined
    d. Undefined

78. In mathematics, the _____ inverse, or opposite, of a number n is the number that, when added to n, yields zero. The _____ inverse of n is denoted −n.
    a. Additive0
    b. Thing
    c. Undefined
    d. Undefined

79. _____ is the distance around a given two-dimensional object. As a general rule, the _____ of a polygon can always be calculated by adding all the length of the sides together. So, the formula for triangles is P = a + b + c, where a, b and c stand for each side of it. For quadrilaterals the equation is P = a + b + c + d. For equilateral polygons, P = na, where n is the number of sides and a is the side length.
    a. Thing
    b. Perimeter0
    c. Undefined
    d. Undefined

80. In geometry a _____ is a plane figure that is bounded by a closed path or circuit, composed of a finite number of sequential line segments.
    a. Thing
    b. Polygon0
    c. Undefined
    d. Undefined

81. A _____ is one of the basic shapes of geometry: a polygon with three vertices and three sides which are straight line segments.
    a. Triangle0
    b. Thing
    c. Undefined
    d. Undefined

82. A _____ is a polynomial consisting of three terms; in other words, it is the sum of three monomials.
    a. Thing
    b. Trinomial0
    c. Undefined
    d. Undefined

83. The metre (or _____, see spelling differences) is a measure of length. It is the basic unit of length in the metric system and in the International System of Units (SI), used around the world for general and scientific purposes.
    a. Meter0
    b. Concept
    c. Undefined
    d. Undefined

84. The term _____ can refer to an integer which is the square of some other integer, or an algebraic expression that can be factored as the square of some other expression.

Chapter 4. POLYNOMIALS AND PROPERTIES OF EXPONENTS

a. Perfect square0
b. Thing
c. Undefined
d. Undefined

85. The _____ is a property of multiplication or addition where the product or sum remains the same, regardless of whether or not the order of the addends or factors are changed.
   a. Commutative property0
   b. Thing
   c. Undefined
   d. Undefined

86. In botany, _____ are above-ground plant organs specialized for photosynthesis. Their characteristics are typically analyzed by using Fiobonacci's sequences.
   a. Thing
   b. Leaves0
   c. Undefined
   d. Undefined

87. In algebra, a _____ is a binomial formed by taking the opposite of the second term of a binomial.
   a. Thing
   b. Conjugate0
   c. Undefined
   d. Undefined

88. In mathematics, a _____ is a mathematical statement which appears likely to be true, but has not been formally proven to be true under the rules of mathematical logic.
   a. Conjecture0
   b. Concept
   c. Undefined
   d. Undefined

89. In geometry, a _____ is defined as a quadrilateral where all four of its angles are right angles.
   a. Rectangle0
   b. Thing
   c. Undefined
   d. Undefined

90. In mathematics, _____ geometry was the traditional name for the geometry of three-dimensional Euclidean space — for practical purposes the kind of space we live in.
   a. Solid0
   b. Thing
   c. Undefined
   d. Undefined

91. In mathematics, a _____ of an integer n, also called a factor of n, is an integer which evenly divides n without leaving a remainder.
   a. Thing
   b. Divisor0
   c. Undefined
   d. Undefined

92. In arithmetic, _____ is a procedure for calculating the division of one integer, called the dividend, by another integer called the divisor, to produce a result called the quotient.
   a. Thing
   b. Long division0
   c. Undefined
   d. Undefined

93. _____ is a payment made by a company to its shareholders
   a. Thing
   b. Dividend0
   c. Undefined
   d. Undefined

Chapter 4. POLYNOMIALS AND PROPERTIES OF EXPONENTS

94. A _____ is a negotiable instrument instructing a financial institution to pay a specific amount of a specific currency from a specific demand account held in the maker/depositor's name with that institution. Both the maker and payee may be natural persons or legal entities.
   a. Thing
   b. Check0
   c. Undefined
   d. Undefined

95. A _____ is the part of the dividend that is left over when the dividend is not evenly divisible by the divisor.
   a. Remainder0
   b. Thing
   c. Undefined
   d. Undefined

96. _____ are the basic objects of study in graph theory. Informally speaking, a graph is a set of objects called points, nodes, or vertices connected by links called lines or edges.
   a. Graphs0
   b. Thing
   c. Undefined
   d. Undefined

97. _____ systems represent systems whose behavior is not expressible as a sum of the behaviors of its descriptors.
   a. Nonlinear0
   b. Thing
   c. Undefined
   d. Undefined

98. The word _____ comes from the Latin word linearis, which means created by lines.
   a. Linear0
   b. Thing
   c. Undefined
   d. Undefined

99. A _____ is an equation in which each term is either a constant or the product of a constant times the first power of a variable.
   a. Linear equation0
   b. Thing
   c. Undefined
   d. Undefined

100. A _____ is a set of numbers that designate location in a given reference system, such as x,y in a planar _____ system or an x,y,z in a three-dimensional _____ system.
   a. Thing
   b. Coordinate0
   c. Undefined
   d. Undefined

101. In mathematics and its applications, a _____ is a system for assigning an n-tuple of numbers or scalars to each point in an n-dimensional space.
   a. Coordinate system0
   b. Concept
   c. Undefined
   d. Undefined

102. _____ is a temperature scale named after the German physicist Daniel Gabriel _____ , who proposed it in 1724.
   a. Thing
   b. Fahrenheit0
   c. Undefined
   d. Undefined

103. _____ is a physical property of a system that underlies the common notions of hot and cold; something that is hotter has the greater _____.

Chapter 4. POLYNOMIALS AND PROPERTIES OF EXPONENTS

   a. Thing
   c. Undefined
   b. Temperature0
   d. Undefined

104. An _____ is a collection of two not necessarily distinct objects, one of which is distinguished as the first coordinate and the other as the second coordinate.
   a. Thing
   c. Undefined
   b. Ordered pair0
   d. Undefined

105. An _____ is an increase, either of some fixed amount, for example added regularly, or of a variable amount.
   a. Thing
   c. Undefined
   b. Increment0
   d. Undefined

106. _____ of an object is its speed in a particular direction.
   a. Velocity0
   c. Undefined
   b. Thing
   d. Undefined

107. A _____ is a vehicle, missile or aircraft which obtains thrust by the reaction to the ejection of fast moving fluid from within a _____ engine.
   a. Thing
   c. Undefined
   b. Rocket0
   d. Undefined

108. _____ are activities that are governed by a set of rules or customs and often engaged in competitively.
   a. Sports0
   c. Undefined
   b. Thing
   d. Undefined

109. In mathematics, the conjugate _____ or adjoint matrix of an m-by-n matrix A with complex entries is the n-by-m matrix A* obtained from A by taking the transpose and then taking the complex conjugate of each entry.
   a. Pairs0
   c. Undefined
   b. Thing
   d. Undefined

110. In mathematics, the concept of a _____ tries to capture the intuitive idea of a geometrical one-dimensional and continuous object. A simple example is the circle.
   a. Curve0
   c. Undefined
   b. Thing
   d. Undefined

111. In astronomy, geography, geometry and related sciences and contexts, a plane is said to be _____ at a given point if it is locally perpendicular to the gradient of the gravity field, i.e., with the direction of the gravitational force at that point.
   a. Horizontal0
   c. Undefined
   b. Thing
   d. Undefined

112. _____ primarily refers to social welfare service concerned with social protection, or protection against socially recognized conditions, including poverty, old age, disability, unemployment, families with children and others.
   a. Thing
   c. Undefined
   b. Social security0
   d. Undefined

Chapter 4. POLYNOMIALS AND PROPERTIES OF EXPONENTS

113. In Euclidean geometry, a _____ is the set of all points in a plane at a fixed distance, called the radius, from a given point, the center.
    a. Thing
    b. Circle0
    c. Undefined
    d. Undefined

114. In physics, an _____ is the path that an object makes around another object while under the influence of a source of centripetal force, such as gravity.
    a. Thing
    b. Orbit0
    c. Undefined
    d. Undefined

115. A _____, as defined by the International Astronomical Union, is a celestial body orbiting a star or stellar remnant that is massive enough to be rounded by its own gravity, not massive enough to cause thermonuclear fusion in its core, and has cleared its neighboring region of planetesimals.
    a. Thing
    b. Planet0
    c. Undefined
    d. Undefined

116. In mathematics, a _____ can mean either an element of the set {1, 2, 3, ...} (i.e the positive integers or the counting numbers) or an element of the set {0, 1, 2, 3, ...} (i.e. the non-negative integers).
    a. Natural number0
    b. Thing
    c. Undefined
    d. Undefined

117. In mathematics, a _____ of a number x is a number r such that $r^2 = x$, or in words, a number r whose square (the result of multiplying the number by itself) is x.
    a. Square root0
    b. Thing
    c. Undefined
    d. Undefined

118. In mathematics, a _____ of a complex-valued function f is a member x of the domain of f such that f(x) vanishes at x, that is, x : f (x) = 0.
    a. Thing
    b. Root0
    c. Undefined
    d. Undefined

119. The payment of _____ as remuneration for services rendered or products sold is a common way to reward sales people.
    a. Thing
    b. Commission0
    c. Undefined
    d. Undefined

120. In geometry, _____ angles are angles that have a common ray coming out of the vertex going between two other rays.
    a. Adjacent0
    b. Concept
    c. Undefined
    d. Undefined

121. A _____ is a one-dimensional picture in which the integers are shown as specially-marked points evenly spaced on a line.
    a. Number line0
    b. Thing
    c. Undefined
    d. Undefined

Chapter 4. POLYNOMIALS AND PROPERTIES OF EXPONENTS

122. A _____ is a set of possible values that a variable can take on in order to satisfy a given set of conditions, which may include equations and inequalities.
   a. Solution set0
   b. Thing
   c. Undefined
   d. Undefined

123. In elementary algebra, an _____ is a set that contains every real number between two indicated numbers and may contain the two numbers themselves.
   a. Interval0
   b. Thing
   c. Undefined
   d. Undefined

124. _____ is the notation in which permitted values for a variable are expressed as ranging over a certain interval; "5 < x < 9" is an example of the application of _____.
   a. Interval notation0
   b. Thing
   c. Undefined
   d. Undefined

Chapter 5. FACTORING POLYNOMIALS

1. In abstract algebra, _____ consists of sets with binary operations that satisfy certain axioms.
   a. Thing
   b. Grouping0
   c. Undefined
   d. Undefined

2. _____ is the largest positive integer that divides both numbers without remainder.
   a. Common Factor0
   b. Thing
   c. Undefined
   d. Undefined

3. In mathematics, _____ is the decomposition of an object into a product of other objects, or factors, which when multiplied together give the original.
   a. Thing
   b. Factoring0
   c. Undefined
   d. Undefined

4. In mathematics, a _____ is the result of multiplying, or an expression that identifies factors to be multiplied.
   a. Product0
   b. Thing
   c. Undefined
   d. Undefined

5. The _____ are the only integral domain whose positive elements are well-ordered, and in which order is preserved by addition. Like the natural numbers, the _____ form a countably infinite set. The set of all _____ is usually denoted in mathematics by a boldface Z .
   a. Thing
   b. Integers0
   c. Undefined
   d. Undefined

6. The _____, the average in everyday English, which is also called the arithmetic _____ (and is distinguished from the geometric _____ or harmonic _____). The average is also called the sample _____. The expected value of a random variable, which is also called the population _____.
   a. Thing
   b. Mean0
   c. Undefined
   d. Undefined

7. In mathematics, a _____ is an expression that is constructed from one or more variables and constants, using only the operations of addition, subtraction, multiplication, and constant positive whole number exponents. is a _____. Note in particular that division by an expression containing a variable is not in general allowed in polynomials. [1]
   a. Polynomial0
   b. Thing
   c. Undefined
   d. Undefined

8. In mathematics, the _____ divisor of two non-zero integers, is the largest positive integer that divides both numbers without remainder.
   a. Greatest common0
   b. Thing
   c. Undefined
   d. Undefined

9. In Math the greates common divisor sometimes known as the _____ of two non- zero integers.
   a. Thing
   b. Greatest common factor0
   c. Undefined
   d. Undefined

10. In mathematics, factorization (British English: factorisation) or factoring is the decomposition of an object (for example, a number, a polynomial, or a matrix) into a product of other objects, or _____, which when multiplied together give the original.

Chapter 5. FACTORING POLYNOMIALS

a. Factors0
b. Thing
c. Undefined
d. Undefined

11. _____ is a natural number that has exactly two distinct natural number divisors, which are 1 and the _____ itself.
   a. Prime number0
   b. Thing
   c. Undefined
   d. Undefined

12. _____, in number theory is the process of breaking down a composite number into smaller non-trivial divisors, which when multiplied together equal the original integer.
   a. Thing
   b. Integer factorization0
   c. Undefined
   d. Undefined

13. In mathematics, a _____ number (or a _____) is a natural number that has exactly two (distinct) natural number divisors, which are 1 and the _____ number itself.
   a. Thing
   b. Prime0
   c. Undefined
   d. Undefined

14. In mathematics, the _____ of two non-zero integers, is the largest positive integer that divides both numbers without remainder.
   a. Thing
   b. Greatest common divisor0
   c. Undefined
   d. Undefined

15. In mathematics, a _____ is a particular kind of polynomial, having just one term.
   a. Monomial0
   b. Thing
   c. Undefined
   d. Undefined

16. In elementary algebra, a _____ is a polynomial with two terms: the sum of two monomials. It is the simplest kind of polynomial except for a monomial.
   a. Thing
   b. Binomial0
   c. Undefined
   d. Undefined

17. An _____ is a combination of numbers, operators, grouping symbols and/or free variables and bound variables arranged in a meaningful way which can be evaluated..
   a. Thing
   b. Expression0
   c. Undefined
   d. Undefined

18. _____ has many meanings, most of which simply .
   a. Thing
   b. Power0
   c. Undefined
   d. Undefined

19. In mathematics, and in particular in abstract algebra, the _____ is a property of binary operations that generalises the distributive law from elementary algebra.
   a. Thing
   b. Distributive property0
   c. Undefined
   d. Undefined

Chapter 5. FACTORING POLYNOMIALS

20. A _____ is a negotiable instrument instructing a financial institution to pay a specific amount of a specific currency from a specific demand account held in the maker/depositor's name with that institution. Both the maker and payee may be natural persons or legal entities.
    a. Thing
    b. Check0
    c. Undefined
    d. Undefined

21. _____, either of the curved-bracket punctuation marks that together make a set of _____
    a. Thing
    b. Parentheses0
    c. Undefined
    d. Undefined

22. In mathematics, a _____ is a constant multiplicative factor of a certain object. The object can be such things as a variable, a vector, a function, etc. For example, the _____ of $9x^2$ is 9.
    a. Thing
    b. Coefficient0
    c. Undefined
    d. Undefined

23. In mathematics, the additive inverse, or _____ of a number n is the number that, when added to n, yields zero. The additive inverse of n is denoted −n. For example, 7 is −7, because 7 + (−7) = 0, and the additive inverse of −0.3 is 0.3, because −0.3 + 0.3 = 0.
    a. Thing
    b. Opposite0
    c. Undefined
    d. Undefined

24. In mathematics, the _____ of a number n is the number that, when added to n, yields zero. The _____ of n is denoted −n. For example, 7 is −7, because 7 + (−7) = 0, and the _____ of −0.3 is 0.3, because −0.3 + 0.3 = 0.
    a. Additive inverse0
    b. Thing
    c. Undefined
    d. Undefined

25. A _____ is a polynomial consisting of three terms; in other words, it is the sum of three monomials.
    a. Trinomial0
    b. Thing
    c. Undefined
    d. Undefined

26. In mathematics, _____ expressions is used to reduce the expression into the lowest possible term.
    a. Simplifying0
    b. Thing
    c. Undefined
    d. Undefined

27. In mathematics, _____ is an elementary arithmetic operation. When one of the numbers is a whole number, _____ is the repeated sum of the other number.
    a. Thing
    b. Multiplication0
    c. Undefined
    d. Undefined

28. Equivalence is the condition of being _____ or essentially equal.
    a. Equivalent0
    b. Thing
    c. Undefined
    d. Undefined

29. A _____ is a four-sided plane figure that has two sets of opposite parallel sides.

Chapter 5. FACTORING POLYNOMIALS

a. Parallelogram0
b. Concept
c. Undefined
d. Undefined

30. _____ is the distance around a given two-dimensional object. As a general rule, the _____ of a polygon can always be calculated by adding all the length of the sides together. So, the formula for triangles is P = a + b + c, where a, b and c stand for each side of it. For quadrilaterals the equation is P = a + b + c + d. For equilateral polygons, P = na, where n is the number of sides and a is the side length.
a. Perimeter0
b. Thing
c. Undefined
d. Undefined

31. In geometry, _____ angles are angles that have a common ray coming out of the vertex going between two other rays.
a. Adjacent0
b. Concept
c. Undefined
d. Undefined

32. In classical geometry, a _____ of a circle or sphere is any line segment from its center to its boundary. By extension, the _____ of a circle or sphere is the length of any such segment. The _____ is half the diameter. In science and engineering the term _____ of curvature is commonly used as a synonym for _____.
a. Thing
b. Radius0
c. Undefined
d. Undefined

33. In mathematics, a _____ is a quadric surface, with the following equation in Cartesian coordinates: $(x/_a)^2 + (y/_b)^2 = 1$.
a. Cylinder0
b. Thing
c. Undefined
d. Undefined

34. A _____ is a special kind of ratio, indicating a relationship between two measurements with different units, such as miles to gallons or cents to pounds.
a. Thing
b. Rate0
c. Undefined
d. Undefined

35. _____ is a kind of property which exists as magnitude or multitude. It is among the basic classes of things along with quality, substance, change, and relation.
a. Amount0
b. Thing
c. Undefined
d. Undefined

36. _____ is the fee paid on borrowed money.
a. Interest0
b. Thing
c. Undefined
d. Undefined

37. A _____ is the result of the addition of a set of numbers. The numbers may be natural numbers, complex numbers, matrices, or still more complicated objects. An infinite _____ is a subtle procedure known as a series.
a. Sum0
b. Thing
c. Undefined
d. Undefined

Chapter 5. FACTORING POLYNOMIALS

38. In mathematics and the mathematical sciences, a _____ is a fixed, but possibly unspecified, value. This is in contrast to a variable, which is not fixed.
   a. Thing
   b. Constant0
   c. Undefined
   d. Undefined

39. In mathematics, the conjugate _____ or adjoint matrix of an m-by-n matrix A with complex entries is the n-by-m matrix A* obtained from A by taking the transpose and then taking the complex conjugate of each entry.
   a. Pairs0
   b. Thing
   c. Undefined
   d. Undefined

40. In combinatorial mathematics, a _____ is an un-ordered collection of unique elements.
   a. Combination0
   b. Concept
   c. Undefined
   d. Undefined

41. Acid _____ ratio measures the ability of a company to use its near cash or quick assets to immediately extinguish its current liabilities.
   a. Test0
   b. Thing
   c. Undefined
   d. Undefined

42. _____ the expected value of a random variable displays the average or central value of the variable. It is a summary value of the distribution of the variable.
   a. Thing
   b. Determining0
   c. Undefined
   d. Undefined

43. In mathematics, an inequality is a statement about the relative size or order of two objects. For example 14 > 10, or 14 is _____ 10.
   a. Thing
   b. Greater than0
   c. Undefined
   d. Undefined

44. A _____ of a number is the product of that number with any integer.
   a. Multiple0
   b. Thing
   c. Undefined
   d. Undefined

45. In plane geometry, a _____ is a polygon with four equal sides, four right angles, and parallel opposite sides. In algebra, the _____ of a number is that number multiplied by itself.
   a. Square0
   b. Thing
   c. Undefined
   d. Undefined

46. The term _____ can refer to an integer which is the square of some other integer, or an algebraic expression that can be factored as the square of some other expression.
   a. Thing
   b. Perfect square0
   c. Undefined
   d. Undefined

47. In algebra, a _____ is a binomial formed by taking the opposite of the second term of a binomial.

Chapter 5. FACTORING POLYNOMIALS

a. Conjugate0
c. Undefined
b. Thing
d. Undefined

48. A _____ is a symbolic representation denoting a quantity or expression. It often represents an "unknown" quantity that has the potential to change.
   a. Thing
   b. Variable0
   c. Undefined
   d. Undefined

49. _____ is a concept that permeates much of inferential statistics and descriptive statistics. More properly, it is "the sum of the squared deviations".
   a. Sum of squares0
   b. Thing
   c. Undefined
   d. Undefined

50. A _____ is a three-dimensional solid object bounded by six square faces, facets, or sides, with three meeting at each vertex.
   a. Thing
   b. Cube0
   c. Undefined
   d. Undefined

51. _____ are of a number n in its third power-the result of multiplying it by itself three times.
   a. Cubes0
   b. Thing
   c. Undefined
   d. Undefined

52. A _____ is a number which is the cube of an integer.
   a. Perfect cube0
   b. Thing
   c. Undefined
   d. Undefined

53. _____ is a mathematical operation, written a^n, involving two numbers, the base a and the exponent n.
   a. Exponentiating0
   b. Thing
   c. Undefined
   d. Undefined

54. _____ is a mathematical operation, written a^n, involving two numbers, the base a and the exponent n.
   a. Exponentiation0
   b. Thing
   c. Undefined
   d. Undefined

55. In mathematics, a _____ of an integer n, also called a factor of n, is an integer which evenly divides n without leaving a remainder.
   a. Thing
   b. Divisor0
   c. Undefined
   d. Undefined

56. In mathematics, there are several meanings of _____ depending on the subject.
   a. Degree0
   b. Thing
   c. Undefined
   d. Undefined

57. In arithmetic, _____ is a procedure for calculating the division of one integer, called the dividend, by another integer called the divisor, to produce a result called the quotient.

Chapter 5. FACTORING POLYNOMIALS

a. Thing
c. Undefined
b. Long division0
d. Undefined

58. The _____ governs the differentiation of products of differentiable functions.
   a. Thing
   c. Undefined
   b. Product rule0
   d. Undefined

59. In mathematics, a _____ is a polynomial equation of the second degree. The general form is $ax^2 + bx + c = 0$.
   a. Thing
   c. Undefined
   b. Quadratic equation0
   d. Undefined

60. The word _____ comes from the Latin word linearis, which means created by lines.
   a. Thing
   c. Undefined
   b. Linear0
   d. Undefined

61. A _____ is an equation in which each term is either a constant or the product of a constant times the first power of a variable.
   a. Thing
   c. Undefined
   b. Linear equation0
   d. Undefined

62. A _____ is one of the basic shapes of geometry: a polygon with three vertices and three sides which are straight line segments.
   a. Triangle0
   c. Undefined
   b. Thing
   d. Undefined

63. _____ over a given field is a polynomial with coefficients in that field.
   a. Algebraic equation0
   c. Undefined
   b. Thing
   d. Undefined

64. _____ is a relation in Euclidean geometry among the three sides of a right triangle.
   a. Thing
   c. Undefined
   b. Pythagorean Theorem0
   d. Undefined

65. _____ has one 90° internal angle a right angle.
   a. Thing
   c. Undefined
   b. Right triangle0
   d. Undefined

66. In mathematics, a _____ is a statement that can be proved on the basis of explicitly stated or previously agreed assumptions.
   a. Thing
   c. Undefined
   b. Theorem0
   d. Undefined

67. _____ was an Greek philosopher. He is best known for a theorem in trigonometry that bears his name.
   a. Pythagoras0
   c. Undefined
   b. Person
   d. Undefined

Chapter 5. FACTORING POLYNOMIALS

68. The _____ of a right triangle is the triangle's longest side; the side opposite the right angle.
    a. Thing
    b. Hypotenuse0
    c. Undefined
    d. Undefined

69. The _____ is that number multiplied by itself.
    a. Thing
    b. Square of a number0
    c. Undefined
    d. Undefined

70. _____ means in succession or back-to-back
    a. Thing
    b. Consecutive0
    c. Undefined
    d. Undefined

71. In the scientific method, an _____ (Latin: ex-+-periri, "of (or from) trying"), is a set of actions and observations, performed in the context of solving a particular problem or question, in order to support or falsify a hypothesis or research concerning phenomena.
    a. Experiment0
    b. Thing
    c. Undefined
    d. Undefined

72. _____, Greek for "knowledge of nature," is the branch of science concerned with the discovery and characterization of universal laws which govern matter, energy, space, and time.
    a. Physics0
    b. Thing
    c. Undefined
    d. Undefined

73. Initial objects are also called _____, and terminal objects are also called final.
    a. Coterminal0
    b. Thing
    c. Undefined
    d. Undefined

74. A _____ is a vehicle, missile or aircraft which obtains thrust by the reaction to the ejection of fast moving fluid from within a _____ engine.
    a. Thing
    b. Rocket0
    c. Undefined
    d. Undefined

75. In geometry a _____, or deltoid, is a quadrilateral with two pairs of congruent adjacent sides.
    a. Kite0
    b. Thing
    c. Undefined
    d. Undefined

76. _____ is the transport of people on a trip/journey or the process or time involved in a person or object moving from one location to another.
    a. Thing
    b. Travel0
    c. Undefined
    d. Undefined

77. A _____ is a unit of length, usually used to measure distance, in a number of different systems, including Imperial units, United States customary units and Norwegian/Swedish mil. Its size can vary from system to system, but in each is between 1 and 10 kilometers. In contemporary English contexts _____ refers to either:

Chapter 5. FACTORING POLYNOMIALS

a. Mile0
b. Thing
c. Undefined
d. Undefined

78. In geometry a _____ is a plane figure that is bounded by a closed path or circuit, composed of a finite number of sequential line segments.
    a. Thing
    b. Polygon0
    c. Undefined
    d. Undefined

79. A _____ can refer to a line joining two nonadjacent vertices of a polygon or polyhedron, or in some contexts any upward or downward sloping line. .
    a. Thing
    b. Diagonal0
    c. Undefined
    d. Undefined

80. In mathematics, the _____ of two sets A and B is the set that contains all elements of A that also belong to B (or equivalently, all elements of B that also belong to A), but no other elements.
    a. Intersection0
    b. Thing
    c. Undefined
    d. Undefined

81. _____ are the basic objects of study in graph theory. Informally speaking, a graph is a set of objects called points, nodes, or vertices connected by links called lines or edges.
    a. Thing
    b. Graphs0
    c. Undefined
    d. Undefined

82. _____ systems represent systems whose behavior is not expressible as a sum of the behaviors of its descriptors.
    a. Thing
    b. Nonlinear0
    c. Undefined
    d. Undefined

83. In business, particularly accounting, a _____ is the time intervals that the accounts, statement, payments, or other calculations cover.
    a. Thing
    b. Period0
    c. Undefined
    d. Undefined

84. A _____ is a set of numbers that designate location in a given reference system, such as x,y in a planar _____ system or an x,y,z in a three-dimensional _____ system.
    a. Coordinate0
    b. Thing
    c. Undefined
    d. Undefined

85. A _____ decimal is a decimal fraction which ends after a definite number of digits.
    a. Thing
    b. Terminating0
    c. Undefined
    d. Undefined

86. _____ represent rational numbers whose fractions in lowest terms are of the form $k/(2^n 5^m)$.
    a. Terminating Decimals0
    b. Thing
    c. Undefined
    d. Undefined

Chapter 5. FACTORING POLYNOMIALS

87. In geographic information systems, a _____ comprises an entity with a geographic location, typically determined by points, arcs, or polygons. Carriageways and cadastres exemplify _____ data.
    a. Thing
    b. Feature0
    c. Undefined
    d. Undefined

88. In linear algebra, the _____ of an n-by-n square matrix A is defined to be the sum of the elements on the main diagonal of A,
    a. Trace0
    b. Thing
    c. Undefined
    d. Undefined

89. _____ are activities that are governed by a set of rules or customs and often engaged in competitively.
    a. Sports0
    b. Thing
    c. Undefined
    d. Undefined

90. _____, from Latin meaning "to make progress", is defined in two different ways. Pure economic _____ is the increase in wealth that an investor has from making an investment, taking into consideration all costs associated with that investment including the opportunity cost of capital.
    a. Thing
    b. Profit0
    c. Undefined
    d. Undefined

91. The _____ is the distance around a closed curve. _____ is a kind of perimeter.
    a. Circumference0
    b. Thing
    c. Undefined
    d. Undefined

92. Mathematical _____ is used to represent ideas.
    a. Thing
    b. Notation0
    c. Undefined
    d. Undefined

93. A _____ is a set of possible values that a variable can take on in order to satisfy a given set of conditions, which may include equations and inequalities.
    a. Thing
    b. Solution set0
    c. Undefined
    d. Undefined

94. In elementary algebra, an _____ is a set that contains every real number between two indicated numbers and may contain the two numbers themselves.
    a. Thing
    b. Interval0
    c. Undefined
    d. Undefined

95. _____ is the notation in which permitted values for a variable are expressed as ranging over a certain interval; "5 < x < 9" is an example of the application of _____.
    a. Interval notation0
    b. Thing
    c. Undefined
    d. Undefined

96. In mathematics, a _____ number is a number which can be expressed as a ratio of two integers. Non-integer _____ numbers (commonly called fractions) are usually written as the vulgar fraction a / b, where b is not zero.

a. Rational0
b. Thing
c. Undefined
d. Undefined

97. In mathematics, an _____, mean, or central tendency of a data set refers to a measure of the "middle" or "expected" value of the data set.
   a. Average0
   b. Concept
   c. Undefined
   d. Undefined

Chapter 6. RATIONAL EXPRESSIONS

1. In mathematics, defined and _____ are used to explain whether or not expressions have meaningful, sensible, and unambiguous values.
   a. Thing
   b. Undefined0
   c. Undefined
   d. Undefined

2. In mathematics, a _____ number is a number which can be expressed as a ratio of two integers. Non-integer _____ numbers (commonly called fractions) are usually written as the vulgar fraction a / b, where b is not zero.
   a. Rational0
   b. Thing
   c. Undefined
   d. Undefined

3. An _____ is a combination of numbers, operators, grouping symbols and/or free variables and bound variables arranged in a meaningful way which can be evaluated..
   a. Expression0
   b. Thing
   c. Undefined
   d. Undefined

4. A _____ is the part of a fraction that tells how many equal parts make up a whole, and which is used in the name of the fraction: "halves", "thirds", "fourths" or "quarters", "fifths" and so on.
   a. Denominator0
   b. Concept
   c. Undefined
   d. Undefined

5. A _____ is a symbolic representation denoting a quantity or expression. It often represents an "unknown" quantity that has the potential to change.
   a. Thing
   b. Variable0
   c. Undefined
   d. Undefined

6. In mathematics, a _____ may be described informally as a number that can be given by an infinite decimal representation.
   a. Thing
   b. Real number0
   c. Undefined
   d. Undefined

7. In mathematics, a _____ of a k-place relation $L \subseteq X_1 \times ... \times X_k$ is one of the sets X_j, $1 \leq j \leq k$. In the special case where k = 2 and $L \subseteq X_1 \times X_2$ is a function $L : X_1 \to X_2$, it is conventional to refer to X_1 as the _____ of the function and to refer to X_2 as the codomain of the function.
   a. Domain0
   b. Thing
   c. Undefined
   d. Undefined

8. Mathematical _____ is used to represent ideas.
   a. Notation0
   b. Thing
   c. Undefined
   d. Undefined

9. A _____ is a numeral used to indicate a count. The most common use of the word today is to name the part of a fraction that tells the number or count of equal parts.
   a. Thing
   b. Numerator0
   c. Undefined
   d. Undefined

10. A _____ is a quantity that denotes the proportional amount or magnitude of one quantity relative to another.

a. Thing
b. Ratio0
c. Undefined
d. Undefined

11. _____ is the largest positive integer that divides both numbers without remainder.
a. Thing
b. Common Factor0
c. Undefined
d. Undefined

12. In mathematics, factorization (British English: factorisation) or factoring is the decomposition of an object (for example, a number, a polynomial, or a matrix) into a product of other objects, or _____, which when multiplied together give the original.
a. Thing
b. Factors0
c. Undefined
d. Undefined

13. A _____ signifies a point or points of probability on a subject e.g., the _____ of creativity, which allows for the formation of rule or norm or law by interpretation of the phenomena events that can be created.
a. Principle0
b. Thing
c. Undefined
d. Undefined

14. In mathematics, a _____ is an expression that is constructed from one or more variables and constants, using only the operations of addition, subtraction, multiplication, and constant positive whole number exponents. is a _____. Note in particular that division by an expression containing a variable is not in general allowed in polynomials. [1]
a. Thing
b. Polynomial0
c. Undefined
d. Undefined

15. In plane geometry, a _____ is a polygon with four equal sides, four right angles, and parallel opposite sides. In algebra, the _____ of a number is that number multiplied by itself.
a. Square0
b. Thing
c. Undefined
d. Undefined

16. Two mathematical objects are equal if and only if they are precisely the same in every way. This defines a binary relation, _____, denoted by the sign of _____ "=" in such a way that the statement "x = y" means that x and y are equal.
a. Thing
b. Equality0
c. Undefined
d. Undefined

17. In common philosophical language, a proposition or _____, is the content of an assertion, that is, it is true-or-false and defined by the meaning of a particular piece of language.
a. Statement0
b. Concept
c. Undefined
d. Undefined

18. In mathematics, _____ is an elementary arithmetic operation. When one of the numbers is a whole number, _____ is the repeated sum of the other number.
a. Thing
b. Multiplication0
c. Undefined
d. Undefined

Chapter 6. RATIONAL EXPRESSIONS

19. An _____ is an equality that remains true regardless of the values of any variables that appear within it, to distinguish it from an equality which is true under more particular conditions.
   a. Identity0
   b. Thing
   c. Undefined
   d. Undefined

20. _____ is a mathematical operation, written a^n, involving two numbers, the base a and the exponent n.
   a. Thing
   b. Exponentiating0
   c. Undefined
   d. Undefined

21. _____ is a mathematical operation, written a^n, involving two numbers, the base a and the exponent n.
   a. Exponentiation0
   b. Thing
   c. Undefined
   d. Undefined

22. In mathematics, the additive inverse, or _____ of a number n is the number that, when added to n, yields zero. The additive inverse of n is denoted −n. For example, 7 is −7, because 7 + (−7) = 0, and the additive inverse of −0.3 is 0.3, because −0.3 + 0.3 = 0.
   a. Opposite0
   b. Thing
   c. Undefined
   d. Undefined

23. In mathematics, the _____ of a number n is the number that, when added to n, yields zero. The _____ of n is denoted −n. For example, 7 is −7, because 7 + (−7) = 0, and the _____ of −0.3 is 0.3, because −0.3 + 0.3 = 0.
   a. Thing
   b. Additive inverse0
   c. Undefined
   d. Undefined

24. Equivalence is the condition of being _____ or essentially equal.
   a. Thing
   b. Equivalent0
   c. Undefined
   d. Undefined

25. In mathematics, an _____, mean, or central tendency of a data set refers to a measure of the "middle" or "expected" value of the data set.
   a. Concept
   b. Average0
   c. Undefined
   d. Undefined

26. A _____ is a landform that extends above the surrounding terrain in a limited area. A _____ is generally steeper than a hill, but there is no universally accepted standard definition for the height of a _____ or a hill although a _____ usually has an identifiable summit.
   a. Thing
   b. Mountain0
   c. Undefined
   d. Undefined

Chapter 6. RATIONAL EXPRESSIONS

27. Fixed costs are expenses whose total does not change in proportion to the activity of a business. Unit fixed costs decline with volume following a retangular hyperbola as the volume of production. Variable costs by contrast change in relation to the activity of a business such as sales or production volume. Along with variable costs, fixed costs make up one of the two components of total cost. In the most simple production function total cost is equal to fixed costs plus variable costs. In accounting terminology, fixed costs will broadly include all costs which are not included in cost of goods sold, and variable costs are those captured in costs of goods sold. The implicit assumption required to make the equivalence between the accounting and economics terminology is that the accounting period is equal to the period in which fixed costs do not vary in relation to production. In practice, this equivalence does not always hold and depending on the period under consideration by management, some overhead expenses can be adjusted by management, and the specific allocation of each expense to each category will be decided under cost accounting. In business planning and management accounting, usage of the terms fixed costs, variable costs and others will often differ from usage in economics, and may depend on the intended use. For example, costs may be segregated into per unit costs fixed costs per period, and variable costs as a proportion of revenue. Capital expenditures will usually be allocated separately, and depending on the purpose, a portion may be regularly allocated to expenses as depreciation and amortization and seen as a _____ per period, or the entire amount may be considered upfront fixed costs.
    a. Thing
    b. Fixed cost0
    c. Undefined
    d. Undefined

28. The _____ of measurement are a globally standardized and modernized form of the metric system.
    a. Units0
    b. Thing
    c. Undefined
    d. Undefined

29. The conversion of units (_____) refers to conversion factors between different units of measurement for the same quantity.
    a. Converting units0
    b. Concept
    c. Undefined
    d. Undefined

30. In mathematics, the multiplicative inverse of a number x, denoted $1/x$ or x^{-1}, is the number which, when multiplied by x, yields 1. The multiplicative inverse of x is also called the _____ of x.
    a. Reciprocal0
    b. Thing
    c. Undefined
    d. Undefined

31. In arithmetic and algebra, when a number or expression is both preceded and followed by a binary operation, an _____ is required for which operation should be applied first.
    a. Thing
    b. Order of operations0
    c. Undefined
    d. Undefined

32. A _____ fraction is a fraction in which the absolute value of the numerator is less than the denominator--hence, the absolute value of the fraction is less than 1.
    a. Thing
    b. Proper0
    c. Undefined
    d. Undefined

33. _____, either of the curved-bracket punctuation marks that together make a set of _____
    a. Thing
    b. Parentheses0
    c. Undefined
    d. Undefined

Chapter 6. RATIONAL EXPRESSIONS 69

34. _____ is the estimation of a physical quantity such as distance, energy, temperature, or time.
   a. Thing
   b. Measurement0
   c. Undefined
   d. Undefined

35. _____ is a concept in traditional logic referring to a "type of immediate inference in which from a given proposition another proposition is inferred which has as its subject the predicate of the original proposition and as its predicate the subject of the original proposition (the quality of the proposition being retained)."
   a. Conversion0
   b. Concept
   c. Undefined
   d. Undefined

36. A _____ is a unit of length, usually used to measure distance, in a number of different systems, including Imperial units, United States customary units and Norwegian/Swedish mil. Its size can vary from system to system, but in each is between 1 and 10 kilometers. In contemporary English contexts _____ refers to either:
   a. Thing
   b. Mile0
   c. Undefined
   d. Undefined

37. The _____ or kilogramme is the SI base unit of mass. It is defined as being equal to the mass of the international prototype of the _____.
   a. Thing
   b. Kilogram0
   c. Undefined
   d. Undefined

38. _____ is electromagnetic radiation with a wavelength that is visible to the eye (visible _____) or, in a technical or scientific context, electromagnetic radiation of any wavelength.
   a. Thing
   b. Light0
   c. Undefined
   d. Undefined

39. _____ is the property of a physical object that quantifies the amount of matter and energy it is equivalent to.
   a. Thing
   b. Mass0
   c. Undefined
   d. Undefined

40. A _____ is a function that assigns a number to subsets of a given set.
   a. Thing
   b. Measure0
   c. Undefined
   d. Undefined

41. In physics, _____ is an influence that may cause an object to accelerate. It may be experienced as a lift, a push, or a pull. The actual acceleration of the body is determined by the vector sum of all forces acting on it, known as net _____ or resultant _____.
   a. Force0
   b. Thing
   c. Undefined
   d. Undefined

42. _____ is a set, with some particular properties and usually some additional structure, such as the operations of addition or multiplication, for instance.
   a. Thing
   b. Space0
   c. Undefined
   d. Undefined

Chapter 6. RATIONAL EXPRESSIONS

43. In physics, an _____ is the path that an object makes around another object while under the influence of a source of centripetal force, such as gravity.
    a. Orbit0
    b. Thing
    c. Undefined
    d. Undefined

44. In geometry, an _____ of a triangle is a straight line through a vertex and perpendicular to (i.e. forming a right angle with) the opposite side or an extension of the opposite side.
    a. Altitude0
    b. Concept
    c. Undefined
    d. Undefined

45. _____ are a measure of time.
    a. Thing
    b. Minutes0
    c. Undefined
    d. Undefined

46. A _____ is a special kind of ratio, indicating a relationship between two measurements with different units, such as miles to gallons or cents to pounds.
    a. Rate0
    b. Thing
    c. Undefined
    d. Undefined

47. _____ is the transport of people on a trip/journey or the process or time involved in a person or object moving from one location to another.
    a. Thing
    b. Travel0
    c. Undefined
    d. Undefined

48. In Euclidean geometry, a uniform _____ is a linear transformation that enlargers or diminishes objects, and whose _____ factor is the same in all directions. This is also called homothethy.
    a. Thing
    b. Scale0
    c. Undefined
    d. Undefined

49. In mathematics a _____ is a function which defines a distance between elements of a set.
    a. Thing
    b. Metric0
    c. Undefined
    d. Undefined

50. A _____ of a number is the product of that number with any integer.
    a. Multiple0
    b. Thing
    c. Undefined
    d. Undefined

51. The _____ of two integers is the smallest positive integer that is a multiple of both intergers.
    a. Thing
    b. Least common multiple0
    c. Undefined
    d. Undefined

52. In mathematics, a _____ is the result of multiplying, or an expression that identifies factors to be multiplied.
    a. Product0
    b. Thing
    c. Undefined
    d. Undefined

53. _____ has many meanings, most of which simply .

Chapter 6. RATIONAL EXPRESSIONS

    a. Thing
    b. Power0
    c. Undefined
    d. Undefined

54. In mathematics, and in particular in abstract algebra, the _____ is a property of binary operations that generalises the distributive law from elementary algebra.
    a. Distributive property0
    b. Thing
    c. Undefined
    d. Undefined

55. A _____ is a negotiable instrument instructing a financial institution to pay a specific amount of a specific currency from a specific demand account held in the maker/depositor's name with that institution. Both the maker and payee may be natural persons or legal entities.
    a. Thing
    b. Check0
    c. Undefined
    d. Undefined

56. In Euclidean geometry, a _____ is moving every point a constant distance in a specified direction.
    a. Translation0
    b. Concept
    c. Undefined
    d. Undefined

57. In mathematics, a _____ is the end result of a division problem. It can also be expressed as the number of times the divisor divides into the dividend.
    a. Quotient0
    b. Thing
    c. Undefined
    d. Undefined

58. _____ is the distance around a given two-dimensional object. As a general rule, the _____ of a polygon can always be calculated by adding all the length of the sides together. So, the formula for triangles is P = a + b + c, where a, b and c stand for each side of it. For quadrilaterals the equation is P = a + b + c + d. For equilateral polygons, P = na, where n is the number of sides and a is the side length.
    a. Perimeter0
    b. Thing
    c. Undefined
    d. Undefined

59. A _____ is the result of the addition of a set of numbers. The numbers may be natural numbers, complex numbers, matrices, or still more complicated objects. An infinite _____ is a subtle procedure known as a series.
    a. Sum0
    b. Thing
    c. Undefined
    d. Undefined

60. In mathematics, _____ expressions is used to reduce the expression into the lowest possible term.
    a. Thing
    b. Simplifying0
    c. Undefined
    d. Undefined

61. In mathematics, a _____ is a polynomial equation of the second degree. The general form is $ax^2 + bx + c = 0$.
    a. Quadratic equation0
    b. Thing
    c. Undefined
    d. Undefined

62. The word _____ comes from the Latin word linearis, which means created by lines.

a. Thing
b. Linear0
c. Undefined
d. Undefined

63. A _____ is an equation in which each term is either a constant or the product of a constant times the first power of a variable.
    a. Thing
    b. Linear equation0
    c. Undefined
    d. Undefined

64. In physics, a _____ may refer to the scalar _____ or to the vector _____.
    a. Thing
    b. Potential0
    c. Undefined
    d. Undefined

65. _____ is a special mathematical relationship between two quantities. Two quantities are called proportional if they vary in such a way that one of the quantities is a constant multiple of the other, or equivalently if they have a constant ratio.
    a. Thing
    b. Proportionality0
    c. Undefined
    d. Undefined

66. _____ (or proportionality) are two quantities that vary in such a way that one of the quatities is a constant multiple of the other, or equivalently if they have a constant ratio.
    a. Proportions0
    b. Thing
    c. Undefined
    d. Undefined

67. _____ is a binary operation on two vectors in a three-dimensional Euclidean space that results in another vector which is perpedicular to the two input vectors.
    a. Thing
    b. Cross product0
    c. Undefined
    d. Undefined

68. _____ traditionally refers to the statistical process of determining comparable scores on different forms of an exam
    a. Equating0
    b. Thing
    c. Undefined
    d. Undefined

69. In sociology and biology a _____ is the collection of people or organisms of a particular species living in a given geographic area or space, usually measured by a census.
    a. Population0
    b. Thing
    c. Undefined
    d. Undefined

70. In mathematics, a _____ is a two-dimensional manifold or surface that is perfectly flat.
    a. Plane0
    b. Thing
    c. Undefined
    d. Undefined

71. _____ is a term applied when talking about the movement of air from one place to the next.
    a. Wind speed0
    b. Thing
    c. Undefined
    d. Undefined

Chapter 6. RATIONAL EXPRESSIONS

72. _____ is a kind of property which exists as magnitude or multitude. It is among the basic classes of things along with quality, substance, change, and relation.
   a. Thing
   b. Amount0
   c. Undefined
   d. Undefined

73. The _____ of a solid object is the three-dimensional concept of how much space it occupies, often quantified numerically.
   a. Volume0
   b. Thing
   c. Undefined
   d. Undefined

74. _____ is a physical property of a system that underlies the common notions of hot and cold; something that is hotter has the greater _____.
   a. Thing
   b. Temperature0
   c. Undefined
   d. Undefined

75. In mathematics and the mathematical sciences, a _____ is a fixed, but possibly unspecified, value. This is in contrast to a variable, which is not fixed.
   a. Constant0
   b. Thing
   c. Undefined
   d. Undefined

76. U.S. liquid _____ is legally defined as 231 cubic inches, and is equal to 3.785411784 litres or abotu 0.13368 cubic feet. This is the most common definition of a _____. The U.S. fluid ounce is defined as 1/128 of a U.S. _____.
   a. Gallon0
   b. Thing
   c. Undefined
   d. Undefined

77. In mathematics, two quantities are called _____ if they vary in such a way that one of the quantities is a constant multiple of the other, or equivalently if they have a constant ratio.
   a. Proportional0
   b. Thing
   c. Undefined
   d. Undefined

78. In geometry a _____ is a plane figure that is bounded by a closed path or circuit, composed of a finite number of sequential line segments.
   a. Thing
   b. Polygon0
   c. Undefined
   d. Undefined

79. In geometry, _____ are plane figures that are bounded by a closed path or circuit, composed of a finite number of sequential line segments.
   a. Polygons0
   b. Thing
   c. Undefined
   d. Undefined

80. A _____ is one of the basic shapes of geometry: a polygon with three vertices and three sides which are straight line segments.
   a. Thing
   b. Triangle0
   c. Undefined
   d. Undefined

Chapter 6. RATIONAL EXPRESSIONS

81. A _____ is a unit of length in the metric system, equal to one thousand metres, the current SI base unit of length
   a. Kilometer0
   b. Thing
   c. Undefined
   d. Undefined

82. In mathematics, a _____ number (or a _____) is a natural number that has exactly two (distinct) natural number divisors, which are 1 and the _____ number itself.
   a. Thing
   b. Prime0
   c. Undefined
   d. Undefined

83. The _____ of a positive integer are the prime numbers that divide into that integer exactly, without leaving a remainder. The process of finding these numbers is called integer factorization, or prime factorization.
   a. Prime factor0
   b. Thing
   c. Undefined
   d. Undefined

84. In mathematics, an _____ is a statement about the relative size or order of two objects.
   a. Inequality0
   b. Thing
   c. Undefined
   d. Undefined

85. A pair of angles are said to be _____ if they share the same vertex and are bounded by the same pair of lines but are opposite to each other. They are also congruent.
   a. Vertical angles0
   b. Thing
   c. Undefined
   d. Undefined

86. _____ is a relation in Euclidean geometry among the three sides of a right triangle.
   a. Pythagorean Theorem0
   b. Thing
   c. Undefined
   d. Undefined

87. _____ has one 90° internal angle a right angle.
   a. Thing
   b. Right triangle0
   c. Undefined
   d. Undefined

88. In mathematics, a _____ is a statement that can be proved on the basis of explicitly stated or previously agreed assumptions.
   a. Theorem0
   b. Thing
   c. Undefined
   d. Undefined

89. In geometry, a _____ is defined as a quadrilateral where all four of its angles are right angles.
   a. Rectangle0
   b. Thing
   c. Undefined
   d. Undefined

Chapter 7. GRAPHING LINEAR EQUATIONS IN TWO VARIABLES

1. A _____ is a symbolic representation denoting a quantity or expression. It often represents an "unknown" quantity that has the potential to change.
   a. Variable0
   b. Thing
   c. Undefined
   d. Undefined

2. The word _____ comes from the Latin word linearis, which means created by lines.
   a. Linear0
   b. Thing
   c. Undefined
   d. Undefined

3. A _____ is an equation in which each term is either a constant or the product of a constant times the first power of a variable.
   a. Thing
   b. Linear equation0
   c. Undefined
   d. Undefined

4. In common philosophical language, a proposition or _____, is the content of an assertion, that is, it is true-or-false and defined by the meaning of a particular piece of language.
   a. Statement0
   b. Concept
   c. Undefined
   d. Undefined

5. An _____ is a collection of two not necessarily distinct objects, one of which is distinguished as the first coordinate and the other as the second coordinate.
   a. Ordered pair0
   b. Thing
   c. Undefined
   d. Undefined

6. A _____ is a set of possible values that a variable can take on in order to satisfy a given set of conditions, which may include equations and inequalities.
   a. Solution set0
   b. Thing
   c. Undefined
   d. Undefined

7. A _____ is a set of numbers that designate location in a given reference system, such as x,y in a planar _____ system or an x,y,z in a three-dimensional _____ system.
   a. Coordinate0
   b. Thing
   c. Undefined
   d. Undefined

8. In mathematics and its applications, a _____ is a system for assigning an n-tuple of numbers or scalars to each point in an n-dimensional space.
   a. Concept
   b. Coordinate system0
   c. Undefined
   d. Undefined

9. A _____ is a negotiable instrument instructing a financial institution to pay a specific amount of a specific currency from a specific demand account held in the maker/depositor's name with that institution. Both the maker and payee may be natural persons or legal entities.
   a. Thing
   b. Check0
   c. Undefined
   d. Undefined

10. In mathematics, the conjugate _____ or adjoint matrix of an m-by-n matrix A with complex entries is the n-by-m matrix A* obtained from A by taking the transpose and then taking the complex conjugate of each entry.

Chapter 7. GRAPHING LINEAR EQUATIONS IN TWO VARIABLES

a. Thing
c. Undefined

b. Pairs0
d. Undefined

11. In astronomy, geography, geometry and related sciences and contexts, a plane is said to be _____ at a given point if it is locally perpendicular to the gradient of the gravity field, i.e., with the direction of the gravitational force at that point.
  a. Horizontal0
  c. Undefined
  b. Thing
  d. Undefined

12. A _____ of a number is the product of that number with any integer.
  a. Multiple0
  c. Undefined
  b. Thing
  d. Undefined

13. In mathematics, the _____ of two sets A and B is the set that contains all elements of A that also belong to B (or equivalently, all elements of B that also belong to A), but no other elements.
  a. Intersection0
  c. Undefined
  b. Thing
  d. Undefined

14. In mathematics, the _____ of a coordinate system is the point where the axes of the system intersect.
  a. Thing
  c. Undefined
  b. Origin0
  d. Undefined

15. Any point where a graph makes contact with an coordinate axis is called an _____ of the graph
  a. Thing
  c. Undefined
  b. Intercept0
  d. Undefined

16. In geometry, an _____ of a triangle is a straight line through a vertex and perpendicular to (i.e. forming a right angle with) the opposite side or an extension of the opposite side.
  a. Concept
  c. Undefined
  b. Altitude0
  d. Undefined

17. _____ is a physical property of a system that underlies the common notions of hot and cold; something that is hotter has the greater _____.
  a. Temperature0
  c. Undefined
  b. Thing
  d. Undefined

18. An _____ is a straight line around which a geometric figure can be rotated.
  a. Thing
  c. Undefined
  b. Axis0
  d. Undefined

19. The metre (or _____, see spelling differences) is a measure of length. It is the basic unit of length in the metric system and in the International System of Units (SI), used around the world for general and scientific purposes.
  a. Meter0
  c. Undefined
  b. Concept
  d. Undefined

20. In mathematics and the mathematical sciences, a _____ is a fixed, but possibly unspecified, value. This is in contrast to a variable, which is not fixed.

Chapter 7. GRAPHING LINEAR EQUATIONS IN TWO VARIABLES

a. Constant0
b. Thing
c. Undefined
d. Undefined

21. _____ systems represent systems whose behavior is not expressible as a sum of the behaviors of its descriptors.
   a. Nonlinear0
   b. Thing
   c. Undefined
   d. Undefined

22. In plane geometry, a _____ is a polygon with four equal sides, four right angles, and parallel opposite sides. In algebra, the _____ of a number is that number multiplied by itself.
   a. Thing
   b. Square0
   c. Undefined
   d. Undefined

23. _____ is the distance around a given two-dimensional object. As a general rule, the _____ of a polygon can always be calculated by adding all the length of the sides together. So, the formula for triangles is P = a + b + c, where a, b and c stand for each side of it. For quadrilaterals the equation is P = a + b + c + d. For equilateral polygons, P = na, where n is the number of sides and a is the side length.
   a. Perimeter0
   b. Thing
   c. Undefined
   d. Undefined

24. _____ is the transport of people on a trip/journey or the process or time involved in a person or object moving from one location to another.
   a. Thing
   b. Travel0
   c. Undefined
   d. Undefined

25. An _____ is when two lines intersect somewhere on a plane creating a right angle at intersection
   a. Axes0
   b. Thing
   c. Undefined
   d. Undefined

26. _____ are procedures that allow people to exchange information by one of several methods.
   a. Communications0
   b. Thing
   c. Undefined
   d. Undefined

27. In mathematics, an _____, mean, or central tendency of a data set refers to a measure of the "middle" or "expected" value of the data set.
   a. Average0
   b. Concept
   c. Undefined
   d. Undefined

28. In economics _____ means before deductions brutto, e.g. _____ domestic or national product, or _____ profit or income
   a. Gross0
   b. Thing
   c. Undefined
   d. Undefined

29. _____ is a form of periodic payment from an employer to an employee, which is specified in an employment contract.

a. Gross pay0 b. Thing
c. Undefined d. Undefined

30. _____ is the amount of time someone works beyond normal working hours.
a. Compensatory time0 b. Thing
c. Undefined d. Undefined

31. _____ is often used to describe the measurement of the steepness, incline, gradient, or grade of a straight line. The _____ is defined as the ratio of the "rise" divided by the "run" between two points on a line, or in other words, the ratio of the altitude change to the horizontal distance between any two points on the line.
a. Thing b. Slope0
c. Undefined d. Undefined

32. In geographic information systems, a _____ comprises an entity with a geographic location, typically determined by points, arcs, or polygons. Carriageways and cadastres exemplify _____ data.
a. Thing b. Feature0
c. Undefined d. Undefined

33. A _____ is a function that assigns a number to subsets of a given set.
a. Thing b. Measure0
c. Undefined d. Undefined

34. A _____ is a quantity that denotes the proportional amount or magnitude of one quantity relative to another.
a. Ratio0 b. Thing
c. Undefined d. Undefined

35. In mathematics, defined and _____ are used to explain whether or not expressions have meaningful, sensible, and unambiguous values.
a. Thing b. Undefined0
c. Undefined d. Undefined

36. In mathematics, an inequality is a statement about the relative size or order of two objects. For example 14 > 10, or 14 is _____ 10.
a. Greater than0 b. Thing
c. Undefined d. Undefined

37. In geometry, two lines or planes if one falls on the other in such a way as to create congruent adjacent angles. The term may be used as a noun or adjective. Thus, referring to Figure 1, the line AB is the _____ to CD through the point B.
a. Thing b. Perpendicular0
c. Undefined d. Undefined

38. The _____ of a geographic location is its height above a fixed reference point, often the mean sea level.
a. Elevation0 b. Thing
c. Undefined d. Undefined

39. A _____ is the sum of a whole number and a proper fraction.

Chapter 7. GRAPHING LINEAR EQUATIONS IN TWO VARIABLES

a. Thing
b. Mixed number0
c. Undefined
d. Undefined

40. In mathematics, the multiplicative inverse of a number x, denoted 1/x or x^{-1}, is the number which, when multiplied by x, yields 1. The multiplicative inverse of x is also called the _____ of x.
a. Reciprocal0
b. Thing
c. Undefined
d. Undefined

41. _____ the expected value of a random variable displays the average or central value of the variable. It is a summary value of the distribution of the variable.
a. Determining0
b. Thing
c. Undefined
d. Undefined

42. The existence and properties of _____ are the basis of Euclid's parallel postulate. _____ are two lines on the same plane that do not intersect even assuming that lines extend to infinity in either direction.
a. Parallel lines0
b. Thing
c. Undefined
d. Undefined

43. In geometry and trigonometry, a _____ is defined as an angle between two straight intersecting lines of ninety degrees, or one-quarter of a circle.
a. Right angle0
b. Thing
c. Undefined
d. Undefined

44. In mathematics, the additive inverse, or _____ of a number n is the number that, when added to n, yields zero. The additive inverse of n is denoted −n. For example, 7 is −7, because 7 + (−7) = 0, and the additive inverse of −0.3 is 0.3, because −0.3 + 0.3 = 0.
a. Opposite0
b. Thing
c. Undefined
d. Undefined

45. In mathematics, the _____ of a number n is the number that, when added to n, yields zero. The _____ of n is denoted −n. For example, 7 is −7, because 7 + (−7) = 0, and the _____ of −0.3 is 0.3, because −0.3 + 0.3 = 0.
a. Additive inverse0
b. Thing
c. Undefined
d. Undefined

46. A _____ is a special kind of ratio, indicating a relationship between two measurements with different units, such as miles to gallons or cents to pounds.
a. Rate0
b. Thing
c. Undefined
d. Undefined

47. In probability theory and statistics, a _____ is a number dividing the higher half of a sample, a population, or a probability distribution from the lower half.
a. Median0
b. Concept
c. Undefined
d. Undefined

Chapter 7. GRAPHING LINEAR EQUATIONS IN TWO VARIABLES

48. _____ is a mathematical science pertaining to the collection, analysis, interpretation or explanation, and presentation of data. It is applicable to a wide variety of academic disciplines, from the physical and social sciences to the humanities.
   a. Statistics0
   b. Thing
   c. Undefined
   d. Undefined

49. A _____ is a unit of length, usually used to measure distance, in a number of different systems, including Imperial units, United States customary units and Norwegian/Swedish mil. Its size can vary from system to system, but in each is between 1 and 10 kilometers. In contemporary English contexts _____ refers to either:
   a. Mile0
   b. Thing
   c. Undefined
   d. Undefined

50. _____ is a notation for writing numbers that is often used by scientists and mathematicians to make it easier to write large and small numbers.
   a. Thing
   b. Scientific notation0
   c. Undefined
   d. Undefined

51. The _____ of measurement are a globally standardized and modernized form of the metric system.
   a. Units0
   b. Thing
   c. Undefined
   d. Undefined

52. _____ are the basic objects of study in graph theory. Informally speaking, a graph is a set of objects called points, nodes, or vertices connected by links called lines or edges.
   a. Thing
   b. Graphs0
   c. Undefined
   d. Undefined

53. _____, in law and economics, is a form of risk management primarily used to hedge against the risk of a contingent loss.
   a. Insurance0
   b. Thing
   c. Undefined
   d. Undefined

54. The _____, the average in everyday English, which is also called the arithmetic _____ (and is distinguished from the geometric _____ or harmonic _____). The average is also called the sample _____. The expected value of a random variable, which is also called the population _____.
   a. Thing
   b. Mean0
   c. Undefined
   d. Undefined

55. _____ are a measure of time.
   a. Thing
   b. Minutes0
   c. Undefined
   d. Undefined

56. In mathematics, a _____ is a constant multiplicative factor of a certain object. The object can be such things as a variable, a vector, a function, etc. For example, the _____ of $9x^2$ is 9.
   a. Coefficient0
   b. Thing
   c. Undefined
   d. Undefined

Chapter 7. GRAPHING LINEAR EQUATIONS IN TWO VARIABLES

57. In geometry, the _____ of an object is a point in some sense in the middle of the object.
   a. Center0
   b. Thing
   c. Undefined
   d. Undefined

58. _____ is the level of functional and/or metabolic efficiency of an organism at both the micro level.
   a. Health0
   b. Thing
   c. Undefined
   d. Undefined

59. In mathematics, an _____ is any of the arguments, i.e. "inputs", to a function. Thus if we have a function f(x), then x is a _____.
   a. Thing
   b. Independent variable0
   c. Undefined
   d. Undefined

60. In a function the _____, is the variable which is the value, i.e. the "output", of the function.
   a. Thing
   b. Dependent variable0
   c. Undefined
   d. Undefined

61. A _____ is a statement or claimt that a particular event will occur in the future in more certain terms than a forecast.
   a. Thing
   b. Prediction0
   c. Undefined
   d. Undefined

62. _____ is a unit of speed, expressing the number of international miles covered per hour.
   a. Miles per hour0
   b. Thing
   c. Undefined
   d. Undefined

63. _____ is a synonym for information.
   a. Data0
   b. Thing
   c. Undefined
   d. Undefined

64. _____ is a kind of property which exists as magnitude or multitude. It is among the basic classes of things along with quality, substance, change, and relation.
   a. Thing
   b. Amount0
   c. Undefined
   d. Undefined

65. _____ is a fixed, but possibly unspecified, value. This is in contrast to a variable, which is not fixed.
   a. Constant term0
   b. Thing
   c. Undefined
   d. Undefined

66. Acid _____ ratio measures the ability of a company to use its near cash or quick assets to immediately extinguish its current liabilities.
   a. Thing
   b. Test0
   c. Undefined
   d. Undefined

Chapter 7. GRAPHING LINEAR EQUATIONS IN TWO VARIABLES

67. _____, usually denoted symbolically by the Greek letter phi, Î¦, gives the location of a place on Earth north or south of the equator. _____ is an angular measurement in degrees (marked with Â°) ranging from 0Â° at the Equator (low _____) to 90Â° at the poles (90Â° N for the North Pole or 90Â° S for the South Pole; high _____). The complementary angle of a _____ is called the colatitude.
   a. Thing
   b. Latitude0
   c. Undefined
   d. Undefined

68. U.S. liquid _____ is legally defined as 231 cubic inches, and is equal to 3.785411784 litres or abotu 0.13368 cubic feet. This is the most common definition of a _____. The U.S. fluid ounce is defined as 1/128 of a U.S. _____.
   a. Thing
   b. Gallon0
   c. Undefined
   d. Undefined

69. _____ is a set, with some particular properties and usually some additional structure, such as the operations of addition or multiplication, for instance.
   a. Thing
   b. Space0
   c. Undefined
   d. Undefined

70. Regrouping is the act of putting ones into groups of 10. For example, the 1 on the far right of 131 would be denoted _____ if the digit of the number being subtracted is larger than 1, such as 131-99.
   a. By 100
   b. Thing
   c. Undefined
   d. Undefined

71. In mathematics, a _____ may be described informally as a number that can be given by an infinite decimal representation.
   a. Real number0
   b. Thing
   c. Undefined
   d. Undefined

72. A _____ is an individual or household that purchases and uses goods and services generated within the economy.
   a. Consumer0
   b. Thing
   c. Undefined
   d. Undefined

73. A _____ is a type of debt. All material things can be lent but this article focuses exclusively on monetary loans. Like all debt instruments, a _____ entails the redistribution of financial assets over time, between the lender and the borrower.
   a. Loan0
   b. Thing
   c. Undefined
   d. Undefined

74. _____ is the symbol used to indicate the nth root of a number
   a. Thing
   b. Radical0
   c. Undefined
   d. Undefined

75. In mathematics, a _____ number is a number which can be expressed as a ratio of two integers. Non-integer _____ numbers (commonly called fractions) are usually written as the vulgar fraction a / b, where b is not zero.

Chapter 7. GRAPHING LINEAR EQUATIONS IN TWO VARIABLES

a. Rational0
b. Thing
c. Undefined
d. Undefined

76. An _____ is a combination of numbers, operators, grouping symbols and/or free variables and bound variables arranged in a meaningful way which can be evaluated..
    a. Thing
    b. Expression0
    c. Undefined
    d. Undefined

77. In mathematics, an _____ number is any real number that is not a rational number- that is, it is a number which cannot be expressed as a fraction m/n, where m and n are integers.
    a. Thing
    b. Irrational0
    c. Undefined
    d. Undefined

78. In mathematics, an _____ is any real number that is not a rational number ¡ª that is, it is a number which cannot be expressed as m/n, where m and n are integers.
    a. Irrational number0
    b. Thing
    c. Undefined
    d. Undefined

79. Mathematical _____ is used to represent ideas.
    a. Thing
    b. Notation0
    c. Undefined
    d. Undefined

80. A pair of angles are _____ if the sum of their angles is 90°.
    a. Concept
    b. Complementary0
    c. Undefined
    d. Undefined

81. In elementary algebra, an _____ is a set that contains every real number between two indicated numbers and may contain the two numbers themselves.
    a. Interval0
    b. Thing
    c. Undefined
    d. Undefined

82. _____ is the notation in which permitted values for a variable are expressed as ranging over a certain interval; "5 < x < 9" is an example of the application of _____.
    a. Interval notation0
    b. Thing
    c. Undefined
    d. Undefined

83. In sociology and biology a _____ is the collection of people or organisms of a particular species living in a given geographic area or space, usually measured by a census.
    a. Population0
    b. Thing
    c. Undefined
    d. Undefined

84. In arithmetic, _____ is a procedure for calculating the division of one integer, called the dividend, by another integer called the divisor, to produce a result called the quotient.
    a. Thing
    b. Long division0
    c. Undefined
    d. Undefined

Chapter 7. GRAPHING LINEAR EQUATIONS IN TWO VARIABLES

85. In mathematics, a _____ is a condition that a solution to an optimization problem must satisfy in order to be acceptable.
   a. Thing
   b. Constraint0
   c. Undefined
   d. Undefined

86. In topology and related areas of mathematics a _____ or Moore-Smith sequence is a generalization of a sequence, intended to unify the various notions of limit and generalize them to arbitrary topological spaces.
   a. Net0
   b. Thing
   c. Undefined
   d. Undefined

87. In mathematics, a _____ is a two-dimensional manifold or surface that is perfectly flat.
   a. Plane0
   b. Thing
   c. Undefined
   d. Undefined

Chapter 8. SYSTEMS OF LINEAR EQUATIONS IN TWO VARIABLES

1. A _____ is a symbolic representation denoting a quantity or expression. It often represents an "unknown" quantity that has the potential to change.
   - a. Variable0
   - b. Thing
   - c. Undefined
   - d. Undefined

2. A _____ is a set of numbers that designate location in a given reference system, such as x,y in a planar _____ system or an x,y,z in a three-dimensional _____ system.
   - a. Coordinate0
   - b. Thing
   - c. Undefined
   - d. Undefined

3. In mathematics and its applications, a _____ is a system for assigning an n-tuple of numbers or scalars to each point in an n-dimensional space.
   - a. Concept
   - b. Coordinate system0
   - c. Undefined
   - d. Undefined

4. The word _____ comes from the Latin word linearis, which means created by lines.
   - a. Thing
   - b. Linear0
   - c. Undefined
   - d. Undefined

5. A _____ is an equation in which each term is either a constant or the product of a constant times the first power of a variable.
   - a. Linear equation0
   - b. Thing
   - c. Undefined
   - d. Undefined

6. _____ is the state of being greater than any finite real or natural number, however large.
   - a. Infinite0
   - b. Thing
   - c. Undefined
   - d. Undefined

7. An _____ is a collection of two not necessarily distinct objects, one of which is distinguished as the first coordinate and the other as the second coordinate.
   - a. Thing
   - b. Ordered pair0
   - c. Undefined
   - d. Undefined

8. In mathematics, the conjugate _____ or adjoint matrix of an m-by-n matrix A with complex entries is the n-by-m matrix A* obtained from A by taking the transpose and then taking the complex conjugate of each entry.
   - a. Thing
   - b. Pairs0
   - c. Undefined
   - d. Undefined

9. In mathematics, the _____ of two sets A and B is the set that contains all elements of A that also belong to B (or equivalently, all elements of B that also belong to A), but no other elements.
   - a. Thing
   - b. Intersection0
   - c. Undefined
   - d. Undefined

10. _____ is often used to describe the measurement of the steepness, incline, gradient, or grade of a straight line. The _____ is defined as the ratio of the "rise" divided by the "run" between two points on a line, or in other words, the ratio of the altitude change to the horizontal distance between any two points on the line.

Chapter 8. SYSTEMS OF LINEAR EQUATIONS IN TWO VARIABLES

  a. Thing
  c. Undefined
  b. Slope0
  d. Undefined

11. _____ the expected value of a random variable displays the average or central value of the variable. It is a summary value of the distribution of the variable.
  a. Determining0
  c. Undefined
  b. Thing
  d. Undefined

12. The existence and properties of _____ are the basis of Euclid's parallel postulate. _____ are two lines on the same plane that do not intersect even assuming that lines extend to infinity in either direction.
  a. Thing
  c. Undefined
  b. Parallel lines0
  d. Undefined

13. Mathematical _____ is used to represent ideas.
  a. Thing
  c. Undefined
  b. Notation0
  d. Undefined

14. A _____ is a set of possible values that a variable can take on in order to satisfy a given set of conditions, which may include equations and inequalities.
  a. Solution set0
  c. Undefined
  b. Thing
  d. Undefined

15. A _____ is the result of the addition of a set of numbers. The numbers may be natural numbers, complex numbers, matrices, or still more complicated objects. An infinite _____ is a subtle procedure known as a series.
  a. Sum0
  c. Undefined
  b. Thing
  d. Undefined

16. _____ are the basic objects of study in graph theory. Informally speaking, a graph is a set of objects called points, nodes, or vertices connected by links called lines or edges.
  a. Thing
  c. Undefined
  b. Graphs0
  d. Undefined

17. In linear algebra, the _____ of an n-by-n square matrix A is defined to be the sum of the elements on the main diagonal of A,
  a. Thing
  c. Undefined
  b. Trace0
  d. Undefined

18. In geographic information systems, a _____ comprises an entity with a geographic location, typically determined by points, arcs, or polygons. Carriageways and cadastres exemplify _____ data.
  a. Feature0
  c. Undefined
  b. Thing
  d. Undefined

19. _____ is a set, with some particular properties and usually some additional structure, such as the operations of addition or multiplication, for instance.

Chapter 8. SYSTEMS OF LINEAR EQUATIONS IN TWO VARIABLES

    a. Thing
    b. Space0
    c. Undefined
    d. Undefined

20. Regrouping is the act of putting ones into groups of 10. For example, the 1 on the far right of 131 would be denoted _____ if the digit of the number being subtracted is larger than 1, such as 131-99.
    a. Thing
    b. By 100
    c. Undefined
    d. Undefined

21. In geometry, the _____ of an object is a point in some sense in the middle of the object.
    a. Center0
    b. Thing
    c. Undefined
    d. Undefined

22. An _____ is a combination of numbers, operators, grouping symbols and/or free variables and bound variables arranged in a meaningful way which can be evaluated..
    a. Thing
    b. Expression0
    c. Undefined
    d. Undefined

23. The _____ is used to discard one of the variables in an equation, only to replace it with the actual value when solving multiple equations.
    a. Substitution method0
    b. Thing
    c. Undefined
    d. Undefined

24. A _____ is a negotiable instrument instructing a financial institution to pay a specific amount of a specific currency from a specific demand account held in the maker/depositor's name with that institution. Both the maker and payee may be natural persons or legal entities.
    a. Check0
    b. Thing
    c. Undefined
    d. Undefined

25. In mathematics, a _____ is a constant multiplicative factor of a certain object. The object can be such things as a variable, a vector, a function, etc. For example, the _____ of $9x^2$ is 9.
    a. Coefficient0
    b. Thing
    c. Undefined
    d. Undefined

26. In mathematics, a _____ may be described informally as a number that can be given by an infinite decimal representation.
    a. Thing
    b. Real number0
    c. Undefined
    d. Undefined

27. An _____ is an equality that remains true regardless of the values of any variables that appear within it, to distinguish it from an equality which is true under more particular conditions.
    a. Identity0
    b. Thing
    c. Undefined
    d. Undefined

28. In common philosophical language, a proposition or _____, is the content of an assertion, that is, it is true-or-false and defined by the meaning of a particular piece of language.

a. Concept
b. Statement0
c. Undefined
d. Undefined

29. A pair of angles is _____ if their respective measures sum to 180 degrees.
   a. Concept
   b. Supplementary0
   c. Undefined
   d. Undefined

30. A _____ is one of the basic shapes of geometry: a polygon with three vertices and three sides which are straight line segments.
   a. Thing
   b. Triangle0
   c. Undefined
   d. Undefined

31. _____ has one 90° internal angle a right angle.
   a. Thing
   b. Right triangle0
   c. Undefined
   d. Undefined

32. Angles smaller than a right angle are called _____ angles (less than 90 degrees).
   a. Concept
   b. Acute0
   c. Undefined
   d. Undefined

33. A pair of angles are _____ if the sum of their angles is 90°.
   a. Concept
   b. Complementary0
   c. Undefined
   d. Undefined

34. A _____ given two distinct points A and B on the _____, is the set of points C on the line containing points A and B such that A is not strictly between C and B.
   a. Ray0
   b. Thing
   c. Undefined
   d. Undefined

35. A _____ is a unit of length, usually used to measure distance, in a number of different systems, including Imperial units, United States customary units and Norwegian/Swedish mil. Its size can vary from system to system, but in each is between 1 and 10 kilometers. In contemporary English contexts _____ refers to either:
   a. Mile0
   b. Thing
   c. Undefined
   d. Undefined

36. A _____ is a special kind of ratio, indicating a relationship between two measurements with different units, such as miles to gallons or cents to pounds.
   a. Rate0
   b. Thing
   c. Undefined
   d. Undefined

37. In mathematics, the additive inverse, or _____ of a number n is the number that, when added to n, yields zero. The additive inverse of n is denoted −n. For example, 7 is −7, because 7 + (−7) = 0, and the additive inverse of −0.3 is 0.3, because −0.3 + 0.3 = 0.
   a. Opposite0
   b. Thing
   c. Undefined
   d. Undefined

Chapter 8. SYSTEMS OF LINEAR EQUATIONS IN TWO VARIABLES

38. _____ is a notation for writing numbers that is often used by scientists and mathematicians to make it easier to write large and small numbers.
   a. Scientific notation0
   b. Thing
   c. Undefined
   d. Undefined

39. The plus and _____ signs are mathematical symbols used to represent the notions of positive and negative as well as the operations of addition and subtraction.
   a. Thing
   b. Minus0
   c. Undefined
   d. Undefined

40. In physics, _____ is an influence that may cause an object to accelerate. It may be experienced as a lift, a push, or a pull. The actual acceleration of the body is determined by the vector sum of all forces acting on it, known as net _____ or resultant _____.
   a. Thing
   b. Force0
   c. Undefined
   d. Undefined

41. A _____ is a function that assigns a number to subsets of a given set.
   a. Thing
   b. Measure0
   c. Undefined
   d. Undefined

42. _____ is the fee paid on borrowed money.
   a. Interest0
   b. Thing
   c. Undefined
   d. Undefined

43. In chemistry, a _____ is substance made by combining two or more different materials in such a way that no chemical reaction occurs.
   a. Mixture0
   b. Thing
   c. Undefined
   d. Undefined

44. _____ or investing is a term with several closely-related meanings in business management, finance and economics, related to saving or deferring consumption.
   a. Thing
   b. Investment0
   c. Undefined
   d. Undefined

45. _____ is a kind of property which exists as magnitude or multitude. It is among the basic classes of things along with quality, substance, change, and relation.
   a. Amount0
   b. Thing
   c. Undefined
   d. Undefined

46. _____ is the transport of people on a trip/journey or the process or time involved in a person or object moving from one location to another.
   a. Travel0
   b. Thing
   c. Undefined
   d. Undefined

47. The State of _____ is a state located in the Rocky Mountain region of the United States of America.

Chapter 8. SYSTEMS OF LINEAR EQUATIONS IN TWO VARIABLES

a. Colorado0
b. Thing
c. Undefined
d. Undefined

48. In mathematics, a _____ is a two-dimensional manifold or surface that is perfectly flat.
a. Plane0
b. Thing
c. Undefined
d. Undefined

49. In topology and related areas of mathematics a _____ or Moore-Smith sequence is a generalization of a sequence, intended to unify the various notions of limit and generalize them to arbitrary topological spaces.
a. Net0
b. Thing
c. Undefined
d. Undefined

50. A _____ is a form of collective investment that pools money from many investors and invests their money in stocks, bonds, short-term money market instruments, and/or other securities.
a. Thing
b. Mutual fund0
c. Undefined
d. Undefined

51. In combinatorial mathematics, a _____ is an un-ordered collection of unique elements.
a. Concept
b. Combination0
c. Undefined
d. Undefined

52. In mathematics, an _____ is a statement about the relative size or order of two objects.
a. Inequality0
b. Thing
c. Undefined
d. Undefined

53. Acid _____ ratio measures the ability of a company to use its near cash or quick assets to immediately extinguish its current liabilities.
a. Thing
b. Test0
c. Undefined
d. Undefined

54. In mathematics, _____ geometry was the traditional name for the geometry of three-dimensional Euclidean space — for practical purposes the kind of space we live in.
a. Solid0
b. Thing
c. Undefined
d. Undefined

55. In mathematical analysis and related areas of mathematics, a set is called _____, if it is, in a certain sense, of finite size.
a. Thing
b. Bounded0
c. Undefined
d. Undefined

56. A _____ consists of one quarter of the coordinate plane.
a. Quadrant0
b. Thing
c. Undefined
d. Undefined

57. In geometry, _____ lines are two lines that share one or more common points.

Chapter 8. SYSTEMS OF LINEAR EQUATIONS IN TWO VARIABLES 91

a. Thing
c. Undefined
b. Intersecting0
d. Undefined

58. _____ is a special mathematical relationship between two quantities. Two quantities are called proportional if they vary in such a way that one of the quantities is a constant multiple of the other, or equivalently if they have a constant ratio.
a. Thing
c. Undefined
b. Proportionality0
d. Undefined

59. In economics, _____ describe market relations between prospective sellers and buyers of a good.
a. Thing
c. Undefined
b. Supply and demand0
d. Undefined

60. A _____ is an individual or household that purchases and uses goods and services generated within the economy.
a. Consumer0
c. Undefined
b. Thing
d. Undefined

61. _____ is the largest city in the state of Texas and the fourth-largest in the United States. As of the 2005 U.S. Census estimate, it had a population of more than 2 million.
a. Houston0
c. Undefined
b. Thing
d. Undefined

62. In mathematics, the _____ of a number n is the number that, when added to n, yields zero. The _____ of n is denoted −n. For example, 7 is −7, because 7 + (−7) = 0, and the _____ of −0.3 is 0.3, because −0.3 + 0.3 = 0.
a. Thing
c. Undefined
b. Additive inverse0
d. Undefined

63. In mathematics, an _____, mean, or central tendency of a data set refers to a measure of the "middle" or "expected" value of the data set.
a. Average0
c. Undefined
b. Concept
d. Undefined

64. In geometry, two lines or planes if one falls on the other in such a way as to create congruent adjacent angles. The term may be used as a noun or adjective. Thus, referring to Figure 1, the line AB is the _____ to CD through the point B.
a. Perpendicular0
c. Undefined
b. Thing
d. Undefined

65. In plane geometry, a _____ is a polygon with four equal sides, four right angles, and parallel opposite sides. In algebra, the _____ of a number is that number multiplied by itself.
a. Thing
c. Undefined
b. Square0
d. Undefined

66. In mathematics, a _____ of a number x is a number r such that $r^2 = x$, or in words, a number r whose square (the result of multiplying the number by itself) is x.

a. Square root0
c. Undefined
b. Thing
d. Undefined

67. In mathematics, a _____ of a complex-valued function f is a member x of the domain of f such that f(x) vanishes at x, that is, x : f (x) = 0.
    a. Thing
    c. Undefined
    b. Root0
    d. Undefined

Chapter 9. RADICALS

1. _____ is the symbol used to indicate the nth root of a number
   a. Thing
   b. Radical0
   c. Undefined
   d. Undefined

2. In mathematics, _____ are used to indicate the square root of a number.
   a. Radicals0
   b. Thing
   c. Undefined
   d. Undefined

3. In plane geometry, a _____ is a polygon with four equal sides, four right angles, and parallel opposite sides. In algebra, the _____ of a number is that number multiplied by itself.
   a. Thing
   b. Square0
   c. Undefined
   d. Undefined

4. In mathematics, a _____ of a number x is a number r such that $r^2 = x$, or in words, a number r whose square (the result of multiplying the number by itself) is x.
   a. Square root0
   b. Thing
   c. Undefined
   d. Undefined

5. The _____, the average in everyday English, which is also called the arithmetic _____ (and is distinguished from the geometric _____ or harmonic _____). The average is also called the sample _____. The expected value of a random variable, which is also called the population _____.
   a. Thing
   b. Mean0
   c. Undefined
   d. Undefined

6. In mathematics, a _____ of a complex-valued function f is a member x of the domain of f such that f(x) vanishes at x, that is, $x : f(x) = 0$.
   a. Thing
   b. Root0
   c. Undefined
   d. Undefined

7. A _____ is a number that is less than zero.
   a. Negative number0
   b. Thing
   c. Undefined
   d. Undefined

8. In mathematics, a _____ may be described informally as a number that can be given by an infinite decimal representation.
   a. Thing
   b. Real number0
   c. Undefined
   d. Undefined

9. The _____ integers are all the integers from zero on upwards.
   a. Nonnegative0
   b. Thing
   c. Undefined
   d. Undefined

10. In mathematics, a _____ number is a number which can be expressed as a ratio of two integers. Non-integer _____ numbers (commonly called fractions) are usually written as the vulgar fraction a / b, where b is not zero.
    a. Rational0
    b. Thing
    c. Undefined
    d. Undefined

11. The term _____ can refer to an integer which is the square of some other integer, or an algebraic expression that can be factored as the square of some other expression.
   a. Perfect square0
   b. Thing
   c. Undefined
   d. Undefined

12. In mathematics, an _____ number is any real number that is not a rational number- that is, it is a number which cannot be expressed as a fraction m/n, where m and n are integers.
   a. Thing
   b. Irrational0
   c. Undefined
   d. Undefined

13. In mathematics, an _____ is any real number that is not a rational number ¡ª that is, it is a number which cannot be expressed as m/n, where m and n are integers.
   a. Irrational number0
   b. Thing
   c. Undefined
   d. Undefined

14. In mathematics, _____ are any real number that is not a rational number ¡ª that is, it is a number which cannot be expressed as m/n, where m and n are integers.
   a. Irrational numbers0
   b. Thing
   c. Undefined
   d. Undefined

15. A _____ decimal is a number whose decimal representation eventually becomes periodic (i.e. the same number sequence _____ indefinitely).
   a. Thing
   b. Repeating0
   c. Undefined
   d. Undefined

16. A _____ decimal is a decimal fraction which ends after a definite number of digits.
   a. Thing
   b. Terminating0
   c. Undefined
   d. Undefined

17. The act of _____ is the calculated approximation of a result which is usable even if input data may be incomplete, uncertain, or noisy.
   a. Estimating0
   b. Thing
   c. Undefined
   d. Undefined

18. Equivalence is the condition of being _____ or essentially equal.
   a. Thing
   b. Equivalent0
   c. Undefined
   d. Undefined

19. An _____ is a combination of numbers, operators, grouping symbols and/or free variables and bound variables arranged in a meaningful way which can be evaluated..
   a. Thing
   b. Expression0
   c. Undefined
   d. Undefined

20. The _____ is the number or expression underneath the radical sign.

Chapter 9. RADICALS

a. Radicand0
b. Thing
c. Undefined
d. Undefined

21. The word _____ is used in a variety of ways in mathematics.
    a. Index0
    b. Thing
    c. Undefined
    d. Undefined

22. An _____ of a number a is a number b such that $b^n=a$.
    a. Nth root0
    b. Thing
    c. Undefined
    d. Undefined

23. A _____ is a symbolic representation denoting a quantity or expression. It often represents an "unknown" quantity that has the potential to change.
    a. Variable0
    b. Thing
    c. Undefined
    d. Undefined

24. The _____ (symbol _____) and the millibar (symbol mbar, also mb) are units of pressure.
    a. Thing
    b. Bar0
    c. Undefined
    d. Undefined

25. In mathematics, the _____ (or modulus) of a real number is its numerical value without regard to its sign.
    a. Absolute value0
    b. Thing
    c. Undefined
    d. Undefined

26. A _____ is a three-dimensional solid object bounded by six square faces, facets, or sides, with three meeting at each vertex.
    a. Thing
    b. Cube0
    c. Undefined
    d. Undefined

27. _____ are of a number n in its third power-the result of multiplying it by itself three times.
    a. Cubes0
    b. Thing
    c. Undefined
    d. Undefined

28. A _____ is a number which is the cube of an integer.
    a. Thing
    b. Perfect cube0
    c. Undefined
    d. Undefined

29. A _____ of a number is the product of that number with any integer.
    a. Multiple0
    b. Thing
    c. Undefined
    d. Undefined

30. In Euclidean geometry, a _____ is moving every point a constant distance in a specified direction.
    a. Concept
    b. Translation0
    c. Undefined
    d. Undefined

31. A _____ of a number is a number a such that $a^3 = x$.

a. Cube root
b. Thing
c. Undefined
d. Undefined

32. In mathematics, a _____ is the end result of a division problem. It can also be expressed as the number of times the divisor divides into the dividend.
a. Thing
b. Quotient
c. Undefined
d. Undefined

33. In mathematics, a _____ is the result of multiplying, or an expression that identifies factors to be multiplied.
a. Thing
b. Product
c. Undefined
d. Undefined

34. A _____ is one of the basic shapes of geometry: a polygon with three vertices and three sides which are straight line segments.
a. Thing
b. Triangle
c. Undefined
d. Undefined

35. _____ is a relation in Euclidean geometry among the three sides of a right triangle.
a. Pythagorean Theorem
b. Thing
c. Undefined
d. Undefined

36. _____ has one 90° internal angle a right angle.
a. Right triangle
b. Thing
c. Undefined
d. Undefined

37. In mathematics, a _____ is a statement that can be proved on the basis of explicitly stated or previously agreed assumptions.
a. Thing
b. Theorem
c. Undefined
d. Undefined

38. The _____ governs the differentiation of products of differentiable functions.
a. Thing
b. Product rule
c. Undefined
d. Undefined

39. _____ is the transport of people on a trip/journey or the process or time involved in a person or object moving from one location to another.
a. Thing
b. Travel
c. Undefined
d. Undefined

40. _____ has many meanings, most of which simply .
a. Thing
b. Power
c. Undefined
d. Undefined

41. A _____ is the result of the addition of a set of numbers. The numbers may be natural numbers, complex numbers, matrices, or still more complicated objects. An infinite _____ is a subtle procedure known as a series.

Chapter 9. RADICALS

a. Thing
b. Sum0
c. Undefined
d. Undefined

42. A _____ is a unit of length, usually used to measure distance, in a number of different systems, including Imperial units, United States customary units and Norwegian/Swedish mil. Its size can vary from system to system, but in each is between 1 and 10 kilometers. In contemporary English contexts _____ refers to either:
a. Mile0
b. Thing
c. Undefined
d. Undefined

43. A _____ can refer to a line joining two nonadjacent vertices of a polygon or polyhedron, or in some contexts any upward or downward sloping line. .
a. Thing
b. Diagonal0
c. Undefined
d. Undefined

44. A _____ is a landform that extends above the surrounding terrain in a limited area. A _____ is generally steeper than a hill, but there is no universally accepted standard definition for the height of a _____ or a hill although a _____ usually has an identifiable summit.
a. Mountain0
b. Thing
c. Undefined
d. Undefined

45. A _____ is a unit of length in the metric system, equal to one thousand metres, the current SI base unit of length
a. Thing
b. Kilometer0
c. Undefined
d. Undefined

46. In mathematics, _____ is an elementary arithmetic operation. When one of the numbers is a whole number, _____ is the repeated sum of the other number.
a. Multiplication0
b. Thing
c. Undefined
d. Undefined

47. In mathematics, _____ expressions is used to reduce the expression into the lowest possible term.
a. Simplifying0
b. Thing
c. Undefined
d. Undefined

48. _____ is a branch of mathematics concerning the study of structure, relation and quantity.
a. Algebra0
b. Concept
c. Undefined
d. Undefined

49. In mathematics, factorization (British English: factorisation) or factoring is the decomposition of an object (for example, a number, a polynomial, or a matrix) into a product of other objects, or _____, which when multiplied together give the original.
a. Factors0
b. Thing
c. Undefined
d. Undefined

50. In mathematics, a _____ number (or a _____) is a natural number that has exactly two (distinct) natural number divisors, which are 1 and the _____ number itself.

Chapter 9. RADICALS

    a. Prime0
    c. Undefined
    b. Thing
    d. Undefined

51. The _____ of a positive integer are the prime numbers that divide into that integer exactly, without leaving a remainder. The process of finding these numbers is called integer factorization, or prime factorization.
    a. Thing
    c. Undefined
    b. Prime factor0
    d. Undefined

52. A _____ is a quantity that denotes the proportional amount or magnitude of one quantity relative to another.
    a. Ratio0
    c. Undefined
    b. Thing
    d. Undefined

53. In mathematics, the conjugate _____ or adjoint matrix of an m-by-n matrix A with complex entries is the n-by-m matrix A* obtained from A by taking the transpose and then taking the complex conjugate of each entry.
    a. Pairs0
    c. Undefined
    b. Thing
    d. Undefined

54. In mathematics, and in particular in abstract algebra, the _____ is a property of binary operations that generalises the distributive law from elementary algebra.
    a. Thing
    c. Undefined
    b. Distributive property0
    d. Undefined

55. In mathematics, a _____ is a constant multiplicative factor of a certain object. The object can be such things as a variable, a vector, a function, etc. For example, the _____ of $9x^2$ is 9.
    a. Coefficient0
    c. Undefined
    b. Thing
    d. Undefined

56. The plus and _____ signs are mathematical symbols used to represent the notions of positive and negative as well as the operations of addition and subtraction.
    a. Minus0
    c. Undefined
    b. Thing
    d. Undefined

57. In geometry, a _____ is defined as a quadrilateral where all four of its angles are right angles.
    a. Rectangle0
    c. Undefined
    b. Thing
    d. Undefined

58. _____ is the distance around a given two-dimensional object. As a general rule, the _____ of a polygon can always be calculated by adding all the length of the sides together. So, the formula for triangles is P = a + b + c, where a, b and c stand for each side of it. For quadrilaterals the equation is P = a + b + c + d. For equilateral polygons, P = na, where n is the number of sides and a is the side length.
    a. Perimeter0
    c. Undefined
    b. Thing
    d. Undefined

59. _____ is often used to describe the measurement of the steepness, incline, gradient, or grade of a straight line. The _____ is defined as the ratio of the "rise" divided by the "run" between two points on a line, or in other words, the ratio of the altitude change to the horizontal distance between any two points on the line.

Chapter 9. RADICALS

    a. Thing
    b. Slope0
    c. Undefined
    d. Undefined

60. _____ of an object is its speed in a particular direction.
    a. Thing
    b. Velocity0
    c. Undefined
    d. Undefined

61. Initial objects are also called _____, and terminal objects are also called final.
    a. Thing
    b. Coterminal0
    c. Undefined
    d. Undefined

62. In astronomy, geography, geometry and related sciences and contexts, a plane is said to be _____ at a given point if it is locally perpendicular to the gradient of the gravity field, i.e., with the direction of the gravitational force at that point.
    a. Horizontal0
    b. Thing
    c. Undefined
    d. Undefined

63. The metre (or _____, see spelling differences) is a measure of length. It is the basic unit of length in the metric system and in the International System of Units (SI), used around the world for general and scientific purposes.
    a. Meter0
    b. Concept
    c. Undefined
    d. Undefined

64. Mathematical _____ really refers to two distinct areas of research: the first is the application of the techniques of formal _____ to mathematics and mathematical reasoning, and the second, in the other direction, the application of mathematical techniques to the representation and analysis of formal _____.
    a. Logic0
    b. Thing
    c. Undefined
    d. Undefined

65. In mathematics, a _____ is an expression that is constructed from one or more variables and constants, using only the operations of addition, subtraction, multiplication, and constant positive whole number exponents. is a _____. Note in particular that division by an expression containing a variable is not in general allowed in polynomials. [1]
    a. Thing
    b. Polynomial0
    c. Undefined
    d. Undefined

66. A _____ is a polynomial consisting of three terms; in other words, it is the sum of three monomials.
    a. Trinomial0
    b. Thing
    c. Undefined
    d. Undefined

67. In elementary algebra, a _____ is a polynomial with two terms: the sum of two monomials. It is the simplest kind of polynomial except for a monomial.
    a. Thing
    b. Binomial0
    c. Undefined
    d. Undefined

68. In algebra, a _____ is a binomial formed by taking the opposite of the second term of a binomial.
    a. Conjugate0
    b. Thing
    c. Undefined
    d. Undefined

Chapter 9. RADICALS

69. The _____ is a property of multiplication or addition where the product or sum remains the same, regardless of whether or not the order of the addends or factors are changed.
   a. Commutative property0
   b. Thing
   c. Undefined
   d. Undefined

70. In mathematics, _____ is a property that a binary operation can have. Within an expression containing two or more of the same associative operators in a row, the order of operations does not matter as long as the sequence of the operands is not changed.
   a. Thing
   b. Associativity0
   c. Undefined
   d. Undefined

71. The _____ of a solid object is the three-dimensional concept of how much space it occupies, often quantified numerically.
   a. Volume0
   b. Thing
   c. Undefined
   d. Undefined

72. In geometry, an _____ of a triangle is a straight line through a vertex and perpendicular to (i.e. forming a right angle with) the opposite side or an extension of the opposite side.
   a. Concept
   b. Altitude0
   c. Undefined
   d. Undefined

73. _____ is the SI unit of energy.
   a. Joule0
   b. Thing
   c. Undefined
   d. Undefined

74. The _____ or kilogramme is the SI base unit of mass. It is defined as being equal to the mass of the international prototype of the _____.
   a. Kilogram0
   b. Thing
   c. Undefined
   d. Undefined

75. The _____ of an object is the extra energy which it possesses due to its motion.
   a. Thing
   b. Kinetic energy0
   c. Undefined
   d. Undefined

76. _____ is the property of a physical object that quantifies the amount of matter and energy it is equivalent to.
   a. Thing
   b. Mass0
   c. Undefined
   d. Undefined

77. _____, or Rationalisation in mathematics is the process of removing a square root or imaginary number from the denominator of a fraction.
   a. Thing
   b. Rationalizing0
   c. Undefined
   d. Undefined

78. A _____ is the part of a fraction that tells how many equal parts make up a whole, and which is used in the name of the fraction: "halves", "thirds", "fourths" or "quarters", "fifths" and so on.

Chapter 9. RADICALS

a. Concept
b. Denominator0
c. Undefined
d. Undefined

79. A _____ is a numeral used to indicate a count. The most common use of the word today is to name the part of a fraction that tells the number or count of equal parts.
   a. Numerator0
   b. Thing
   c. Undefined
   d. Undefined

80. _____ is the largest positive integer that divides both numbers without remainder.
   a. Thing
   b. Common Factor0
   c. Undefined
   d. Undefined

81. In mathematics, _____ is the decomposition of an object into a product of other objects, or factors, which when multiplied together give the original.
   a. Thing
   b. Factoring0
   c. Undefined
   d. Undefined

82. _____, either of the curved-bracket punctuation marks that together make a set of _____
   a. Thing
   b. Parentheses0
   c. Undefined
   d. Undefined

83. In mathematics, a _____ is a polynomial equation of the second degree. The general form is $ax^2 + bx + c = 0$.
   a. Thing
   b. Quadratic equation0
   c. Undefined
   d. Undefined

84. A _____ is a negotiable instrument instructing a financial institution to pay a specific amount of a specific currency from a specific demand account held in the maker/depositor's name with that institution. Both the maker and payee may be natural persons or legal entities.
   a. Thing
   b. Check0
   c. Undefined
   d. Undefined

85. In physics, a _____ may refer to the scalar _____ or to the vector _____.
   a. Thing
   b. Potential0
   c. Undefined
   d. Undefined

86. The word _____ comes from the Latin word linearis, which means created by lines.
   a. Linear0
   b. Thing
   c. Undefined
   d. Undefined

87. _____ over a given field is a polynomial with coefficients in that field.
   a. Thing
   b. Algebraic equation0
   c. Undefined
   d. Undefined

88. _____ is a kind of property which exists as magnitude or multitude. It is among the basic classes of things along with quality, substance, change, and relation.

a. Thing
c. Undefined
b. Amount0
d. Undefined

89. _____ is a unit of speed, expressing the number of international miles covered per hour.
    a. Miles per hour0
    b. Thing
    c. Undefined
    d. Undefined

90. Mathematical _____ is used to represent ideas.
    a. Thing
    b. Notation0
    c. Undefined
    d. Undefined

91. _____ is a mathematical operation, written a^n, involving two numbers, the base a and the exponent n.
    a. Thing
    b. Exponentiating0
    c. Undefined
    d. Undefined

92. _____ is a mathematical operation, written a^n, involving two numbers, the base a and the exponent n.
    a. Thing
    b. Exponentiation0
    c. Undefined
    d. Undefined

93. A _____ is a special kind of ratio, indicating a relationship between two measurements with different units, such as miles to gallons or cents to pounds.
    a. Rate0
    b. Thing
    c. Undefined
    d. Undefined

94. _____ is a way of expressing a number as a fraction of 100 per cent meaning "per hundred".
    a. Percent0
    b. Thing
    c. Undefined
    d. Undefined

95. _____ or investing is a term with several closely-related meanings in business management, finance and economics, related to saving or deferring consumption.
    a. Thing
    b. Investment0
    c. Undefined
    d. Undefined

96. _____ is the fee paid on borrowed money.
    a. Thing
    b. Interest0
    c. Undefined
    d. Undefined

97. An _____ is the fee paid on borrow money.
    a. Concept
    b. Interest rate0
    c. Undefined
    d. Undefined

98. In classical geometry, a _____ of a circle or sphere is any line segment from its center to its boundary. By extension, the _____ of a circle or sphere is the length of any such segment. The _____ is half the diameter. In science and engineering the term _____ of curvature is commonly used as a synonym for _____.

Chapter 9. RADICALS

a. Thing
b. Radius0
c. Undefined
d. Undefined

99. In mathematics, a _____ is the set of all points in three-dimensional space (R^3) which are at distance r from a fixed point of that space, where r is a positive real number called the radius of the _____. The fixed point is called the center or centre, and is not part of the _____ itself.
a. Thing
b. Sphere0
c. Undefined
d. Undefined

100. In Euclidean geometry, a _____ is the set of all points in a plane at a fixed distance, called the radius, from a given point, the center.
a. Circle0
b. Thing
c. Undefined
d. Undefined

101. _____ is a state in the southern region of the United States of America and was one of the original Thirteen Colonies that revolted against British rule in the American Revolution.
a. Thing
b. Georgia0
c. Undefined
d. Undefined

102. In mathematics, a _____ is a quadric surface, with the following equation in Cartesian coordinates: $(x/_a)^2 + (y/_b)^2 = 1$.
a. Cylinder0
b. Thing
c. Undefined
d. Undefined

103. _____ is a set, with some particular properties and usually some additional structure, such as the operations of addition or multiplication, for instance.
a. Thing
b. Space0
c. Undefined
d. Undefined

104. The _____ is used to discard one of the variables in an equation, only to replace it with the actual value when solving multiple equations.
a. Thing
b. Substitution method0
c. Undefined
d. Undefined

105. In mathematics, an _____ is a statement about the relative size or order of two objects.
a. Inequality0
b. Thing
c. Undefined
d. Undefined

106. A pair of angles are _____ if the sum of their angles is 90°.
a. Concept
b. Complementary0
c. Undefined
d. Undefined

Chapter 10. FUNCTIONS, COMPLEX NUMBERS, AND QUADRATIC EQUATIONS

1. A _____ is a well-defined collection of objects considered as a whole.
   a. Set10
   b. -equivalence
   c. Undefined
   d. Undefined

2. A measure of variability, the _____ is the distance from the lowest to the highest score.
   a. -equivalence
   b. Range10
   c. Undefined
   d. Undefined

3. _____ is the study of quantity, structure, space, and change. Historically, _____ developed from counting, calculation, measurement, and the study of the shapes and motions of physical objects, through the use of abstraction and deductive reasoning.
   a. -equivalence
   b. Mathematics10
   c. Undefined
   d. Undefined

4. A _____ is an undefined term. However, it is often thought of as a series of points. A _____ has one dimension - length. A _____ is either named by a lower case letter or by two points on the _____.
   a. -equivalence
   b. Line10
   c. Undefined
   d. Undefined

5. The word _____ can have three meanings: In _____ theory, a _____ is an abstract object consisting of vertices (or nodes) and edges (or arcs) between pairs of vertices. The _____ of a function f : X ¨ Y is the set of all pairs (x,f(x)) The _____ of a relation, a generalisation of the _____ of a function.
   a. -equivalence
   b. Graph10
   c. Undefined
   d. Undefined

6. A <U>point </U>is an undefined term. We usually represent this by a dot, but a _____ actually has no dimension. A capital letter names any _____.
   a. Point10
   b. -equivalence
   c. Undefined
   d. Undefined

7. <U>A <U>vertical line </U>goes up and down or from North to South.</U>
   a. -equivalence
   b. Vertical line10
   c. Undefined
   d. Undefined

8. An <U>equation</U> is represented by two expressions that have the same value.
   a. Equation10
   b. ADE classification
   c. Undefined
   d. Undefined

9. A <U>quadratic</U> contains at least one squared term.
   a. -equivalence
   b. Quadratic10
   c. Undefined
   d. Undefined

10. When a value makes an equation true, it is called a <U>solution</U>. 3 is a _____ of x + 2 = 5,
    a. Solution10
    b. -equivalence
    c. Undefined
    d. Undefined

11. _____ are characteristics or properties of an object that can take on one or more different values.

Chapter 10. FUNCTIONS, COMPLEX NUMBERS, AND QUADRATIC EQUATIONS

a. Variables10
b. -equivalence
c. Undefined
d. Undefined

12. An _____ is two numbers, where the first number represents a value on the horizontal axis, and the second number represents a value on the vertical axis, such as (x,y).
   a. ADE classification
   b. Ordered pair10
   c. Undefined
   d. Undefined

13. The bottom part of any fraction represents the number of pieces in one whole unit. This bottom part is called the <U>denominator.</U>
   a. -equivalence
   b. Denominator10
   c. Undefined
   d. Undefined

14. An _____ combines numbers, operators, and/or variables but contains no equal or inequality sign.
   a. ADE classification
   b. Expression10
   c. Undefined
   d. Undefined

15. The very fact that we are measuring objects with respect to some characteristic implies that the objects differ in that characteristic; or stated in another way, that the characteristic can take on a number of different values. These properties or characteristics of an object that can assume two or more different values are referred to as a _____.
   a. -equivalence
   b. Variable10
   c. Undefined
   d. Undefined

16. _____ are intuitively defined as numbers that are in one-to-one correspondence with the points on an infinite line—the number line. The term "real number" is a retronym coined in response to "imaginary number" _____ may be rational or irrational; algebraic or transcendental; and positive, negative, or zero _____ measure continuous quantities. They may in theory be expressed by decimal fractions that have an infinite sequence of digits to the right of the decimal point; these are often (mis-)represented in the same form as 324.823211247... (where the three dots express that there would still be more digits to come, no matter how many more might be added at the end).
   a. Real numbers10
   b. -equivalence
   c. Undefined
   d. Undefined

17. A quadrilateral with 4 equal sides and all right angles is called a <U>square.</U>
   a. Square10
   b. -equivalence
   c. Undefined
   d. Undefined

18. <U>Multiplication</U> is a quick way of adding identical numbers. For example, the sum 7 + 7 + 7 can be found by multiplying 3 times 7. This model is reflected in the use of the word times as a synonym for multiplied by. The resuult of multiplying numbers is called a product. The numbers being multiplied are called factors.
   a. -equivalence
   b. Multiplication10
   c. Undefined
   d. Undefined

19. A _____ is the result of multiplying, or an expression that identifies factors to be multiplied
   a. Product10
   b. -equivalence
   c. Undefined
   d. Undefined

Chapter 10. FUNCTIONS, COMPLEX NUMBERS, AND QUADRATIC EQUATIONS

20. _____ refers to taking a root of a number. _____ 16 means to find the square root of 16, which is 4.
    a. -equivalence
    b. Radical10
    c. Undefined
    d. Undefined

21. _____ (or summation) is one of the basic operations of arithmetic. In its simplest form, _____ combines two numbers, the augend and addend, into a single number, the sum.
    a. ADE classification
    b. Addition10
    c. Undefined
    d. Undefined

22. _____ is one of the four basic arithmetic operations. It is usually denoted by an infix minus sign. The traditional names for the terms of the _____ in the formula c − b = a are minuend (c) − subtrahend (b) = difference (a).
    a. -equivalence
    b. Subtraction10
    c. Undefined
    d. Undefined

23. The answer to subtraction is called the <U>difference</U>.
    a. -equivalence
    b. Difference10
    c. Undefined
    d. Undefined

24. _____ is the property of multiplication over addition which demonstrates that for all numbers a,b,c; a(b+c)=ab+ac, and ab+ac=a(b+c).
    a. Distributive property10
    b. -equivalence
    c. Undefined
    d. Undefined

25. The top part of the fraction is called the <U>numerator</U>. It could also be called the dividend, but _____ is preferred.
    a. Numerator10
    b. -equivalence
    c. Undefined
    d. Undefined

26. When a given number is the product of another number by itself, the another number is called the <U>square root</U>. Ex: 25 = 5 x 5 so 5 is the _____ of 25.
    a. -equivalence
    b. Square root10
    c. Undefined
    d. Undefined

27. A number that does not change in value in a given situation is a _____.
    a. -equivalence
    b. Constant10
    c. Undefined
    d. Undefined

28. A _____ is a number or variable, or the product or quotient of a number or variable.
    a. Term10
    b. -equivalence
    c. Undefined
    d. Undefined

29. A _____ is a multiplicative factor of a certain object such as a variable (for example, the coefficients of a polynomial), a basis vector, a basis function and so on. Usually, the objects and the coefficients are indexed in the same way, leading to expressions such as $a_1x_1 + a_2x_2 + a_3x_3 + \ldots$ where a_n is the _____ of the variable x_n for each n = 1, 2, 3, …

Chapter 10. FUNCTIONS, COMPLEX NUMBERS, AND QUADRATIC EQUATIONS

a. -equivalence
b. Coefficient10
c. Undefined
d. Undefined

30. When two of the same number are multiplied, the result is called a <U>perfect square</U>.
a. -equivalence
b. Perfect square10
c. Undefined
d. Undefined

31. A _____ is simply a polynomial with three terms connect by addition and multiplication.
a. Trinomial10
b. -equivalence
c. Undefined
d. Undefined

32. Whenever a number is raised to the second power, we can also say that the number is _____.
a. -equivalence
b. Squared10
c. Undefined
d. Undefined

33. A <U>quadratic equation </U>is written in standard form as ax^2+ bx + c = 0. In general, a _____ must contain a squared term.
a. -equivalence
b. Quadratic equation10
c. Undefined
d. Undefined

34. A <U>hypotenuse </U>occurs in a right triangle and is the side opposite the right angle. It will also be the longest side of a right triangle.
a. Hypotenuse10
b. -equivalence
c. Undefined
d. Undefined

35. A quadrilateral with opposite sides equal and parallel and containing all right angles is called a <U>rectangle.</U>
a. -equivalence
b. Rectangle10
c. Undefined
d. Undefined

36. A number that is raised to a power, or _____ of an exponential function. This finds common use, for example, in the depiction of numbers, for instance, 10 is the _____ used in the decimal system, whereas 2 is the _____ in the binary numeral system.
a. -equivalence
b. Base10
c. Undefined
d. Undefined

37. Any polygon that has 3 sides is called a <U>triangle</U>.
a. -equivalence
b. Triangle10
c. Undefined
d. Undefined

38. factorization or _____ is the decomposition of an object (for example, a number, a polynomial, or a matrix) into a product of other objects, or factors, which when multiplied together give the original. For example, the number 15 factors into primes as 3 × 5; and the polynomial x2 − 4 factors as (x − 2)(x + 2). In both cases, we obtain a product of simpler things.
a. -equivalence
b. Factoring10
c. Undefined
d. Undefined

39. _____ is used synonymously for variable.

Chapter 10. FUNCTIONS, COMPLEX NUMBERS, AND QUADRATIC EQUATIONS

a. Factor10
b. -equivalence
c. Undefined
d. Undefined

40. The _____ is the term under the radical sign.
a. -equivalence
b. Radicand10
c. Undefined
d. Undefined

41. _____, or less commonly, denary, usually refers to the base 10 numeral system.
a. -equivalence
b. Decimal10
c. Undefined
d. Undefined

42. An <U>axis</U> is one of the number lines found on the rectangular coordinate system. The x asis is the horizontal number line while the y _____ is the vertical number line.
a. ADE classification
b. Axis10
c. Undefined
d. Undefined

43. _____ is implied when data values are distributed in the same way above and below the middle of the sample.
a. Symmetry10
b. -equivalence
c. Undefined
d. Undefined

44. The highest number in a list of values is called the <U>maximum.</U>
a. -equivalence
b. Maximum10
c. Undefined
d. Undefined

45. The _____ is t the point where a graph intersects the y-axis and is found by setting x = 0 and then sovling for the y-value.
a. -equivalence
b. Y-intercept10
c. Undefined
d. Undefined

46. The _____ is the point where a graph intersects the x-axis and is found by letting y = 0 and then solving for the x-value.
a. X-intercept10
b. -equivalence
c. Undefined
d. Undefined

47. An <U>angle</U> is composed of two rays that have a common endpoint, called the vertex. Each _____ is named by a lower case letter or by one point from each ray and the vertex inbetween. _____ a might be the same _____ as _____ ABC.
a. ADE classification
b. Angle10
c. Undefined
d. Undefined

48. The lowest number in a list of values is called the <U>minimum</U>.
a. -equivalence
b. Minimum10
c. Undefined
d. Undefined

Chapter 10. FUNCTIONS, COMPLEX NUMBERS, AND QUADRATIC EQUATIONS

49. A _____ is a concrete example of an item or a specification against which all others may be measured. For example, there are "primary standards" for length, mass (see Kilogram standard), and other units of measure, kept by laboratories and standards organizations.
   a. Standard10
   b. -equivalence
   c. Undefined
   d. Undefined

50. A <U>plane</U> is an undefined term. We can think of it as a series of lines having 2 dimensions, width and length.
   a. Plane10
   b. -equivalence
   c. Undefined
   d. Undefined

51. The <U>radius</U> of a circle is the distance from the center to the circle.
   a. -equivalence
   b. Radius10
   c. Undefined
   d. Undefined

52. A five sided polygon is called a <U>pentagon</U>.
   a. Pentagon10
   b. -equivalence
   c. Undefined
   d. Undefined

53. A measure of central tendency, the _____, corresponds to the point having 50% of the observations below it when observations are arranged in numerical order. The _____ assumes at least an interval level of measurement. For a symmetric distribution such as the normal distribution, the _____ is the same as the mean. For a distribution which is skewed to the right, the _____ is typically smaller than the mean or when skewed to the left, the _____ is smaller.
   a. -equivalence
   b. Median10
   c. Undefined
   d. Undefined

54. The _____ refers to the amount of change in Y for a 1 unit change in X or is the ratio of the rise over the run; or in-other-words, the rate of change in the predicted value as a function of a change in the predictor variable.
   a. Slope10
   b. -equivalence
   c. Undefined
   d. Undefined

Chapter 1

1. b	2. a	3. b	4. a	5. b	6. b	7. a	8. a	9. a	10. a
11. a	12. a	13. b	14. b	15. b	16. b	17. b	18. b	19. b	20. a
21. b	22. a	23. a	24. a	25. a	26. b	27. b	28. b	29. a	30. b
31. b	32. b	33. b	34. b	35. a	36. a	37. b	38. a	39. b	40. a
41. b	42. b	43. b	44. a	45. b	46. a	47. a	48. b	49. b	50. b
51. a	52. a	53. b	54. b	55. b	56. a	57. b	58. b	59. b	60. b
61. a	62. b	63. a	64. b	65. a	66. b	67. a	68. b	69. b	70. a
71. a	72. b	73. a	74. b	75. a	76. b	77. b	78. a	79. b	80. a
81. b	82. a	83. b	84. a	85. a	86. b	87. b	88. a	89. a	90. b
91. b	92. a	93. b	94. b	95. b	96. a	97. a	98. b	99. b	100. a
101. b	102. a	103. b	104. a	105. b	106. a	107. a	108. b	109. b	110. a
111. b	112. b	113. b	114. a						

Chapter 2

1. b	2. b	3. a	4. a	5. a	6. a	7. a	8. a	9. b	10. a
11. a	12. b	13. a	14. a	15. b	16. b	17. a	18. a	19. a	20. a
21. b	22. a	23. b	24. a	25. b	26. b	27. b	28. b	29. a	30. b
31. a	32. a	33. b	34. b	35. a	36. b	37. b	38. b	39. a	40. a
41. b	42. b	43. b	44. b	45. b	46. b	47. b	48. a	49. a	50. a
51. b	52. a	53. b	54. b	55. b	56. b	57. b	58. b	59. b	60. b
61. b	62. a	63. b	64. b	65. a	66. b	67. a	68. b	69. b	70. b
71. a	72. a	73. b	74. b	75. b	76. b	77. a	78. a	79. b	80. a
81. b	82. a	83. a	84. b	85. a	86. a	87. b	88. b	89. a	90. b
91. b	92. b	93. a	94. b	95. b	96. b	97. a	98. b	99. b	100. a
101. b	102. b	103. a	104. a	105. a	106. a	107. b	108. b	109. a	110. b
111. a	112. a								

Chapter 3

1. a	2. a	3. a	4. a	5. a	6. b	7. b	8. a	9. a	10. a
11. b	12. b	13. b	14. a	15. b	16. b	17. a	18. b	19. b	20. b
21. b	22. a	23. a	24. b	25. b	26. a	27. b	28. b	29. b	30. b
31. a	32. a	33. b	34. b	35. a	36. b	37. b	38. b	39. b	40. b
41. b	42. a	43. a	44. b	45. b	46. b	47. a	48. a	49. a	50. b
51. a	52. b	53. a	54. a	55. a	56. b	57. a	58. a	59. a	60. a
61. a	62. b	63. a	64. b	65. a	66. a	67. a	68. a	69. b	70. b
71. b	72. a	73. b	74. b	75. b	76. b	77. b	78. a	79. a	80. b
81. b	82. a	83. a	84. b	85. a	86. b	87. a	88. b	89. a	90. b
91. b	92. a	93. b	94. a	95. a	96. a	97. b	98. a	99. a	100. b
101. b	102. b	103. b	104. a	105. a	106. b	107. a	108. b	109. b	110. a
111. b	112. a	113. b	114. a	115. b	116. b	117. b	118. b	119. a	120. b
121. a	122. b	123. a	124. a	125. b	126. b	127. a	128. a	129. b	130. a
131. b	132. a	133. b	134. a	135. a	136. b	137. b	138. b	139. b	

ANSWER KEY

Chapter 4

1. a	2. a	3. a	4. b	5. a	6. a	7. b	8. a	9. a	10. b
11. b	12. b	13. b	14. b	15. a	16. b	17. b	18. b	19. b	20. a
21. b	22. a	23. a	24. b	25. b	26. a	27. b	28. a	29. a	30. a
31. a	32. b	33. b	34. a	35. a	36. a	37. a	38. a	39. a	40. b
41. a	42. a	43. a	44. b	45. a	46. b	47. b	48. a	49. b	50. a
51. a	52. a	53. b	54. b	55. a	56. a	57. a	58. b	59. b	60. a
61. b	62. b	63. a	64. a	65. a	66. b	67. b	68. a	69. a	70. a
71. a	72. b	73. b	74. b	75. a	76. a	77. b	78. a	79. b	80. b
81. a	82. b	83. a	84. a	85. a	86. b	87. b	88. a	89. a	90. a
91. b	92. b	93. b	94. b	95. a	96. a	97. a	98. a	99. a	100. b
101. a	102. b	103. b	104. b	105. b	106. a	107. b	108. b	109. a	110. a
111. a	112. b	113. b	114. b	115. b	116. a	117. a	118. b	119. b	120. a
121. a	122. a	123. a	124. a						

Chapter 5

1. b	2. a	3. b	4. a	5. b	6. b	7. a	8. a	9. b	10. a
11. a	12. b	13. b	14. b	15. a	16. b	17. b	18. b	19. b	20. b
21. b	22. b	23. b	24. a	25. a	26. a	27. b	28. a	29. a	30. a
31. a	32. b	33. a	34. b	35. a	36. a	37. a	38. b	39. a	40. a
41. a	42. b	43. b	44. a	45. a	46. b	47. a	48. b	49. a	50. b
51. a	52. a	53. a	54. a	55. b	56. a	57. b	58. b	59. b	60. b
61. b	62. a	63. a	64. b	65. b	66. b	67. a	68. b	69. b	70. b
71. a	72. a	73. a	74. b	75. a	76. b	77. a	78. b	79. b	80. a
81. b	82. b	83. b	84. a	85. b	86. a	87. b	88. a	89. a	90. b
91. a	92. b	93. b	94. b	95. a	96. a	97. a			

Chapter 6

1. b	2. a	3. a	4. a	5. b	6. b	7. a	8. a	9. b	10. b
11. b	12. b	13. a	14. b	15. a	16. b	17. a	18. b	19. a	20. b
21. a	22. a	23. b	24. b	25. b	26. b	27. b	28. a	29. a	30. a
31. b	32. b	33. b	34. b	35. a	36. b	37. b	38. b	39. b	40. b
41. a	42. b	43. a	44. a	45. b	46. a	47. b	48. b	49. b	50. a
51. b	52. a	53. b	54. a	55. b	56. a	57. a	58. a	59. a	60. b
61. a	62. b	63. b	64. b	65. b	66. a	67. b	68. a	69. a	70. a
71. a	72. b	73. a	74. b	75. a	76. a	77. a	78. b	79. a	80. b
81. a	82. b	83. a	84. a	85. a	86. a	87. b	88. a	89. a	

Chapter 7

1. a	2. a	3. b	4. a	5. a	6. a	7. a	8. b	9. b	10. b
11. a	12. a	13. a	14. b	15. b	16. b	17. a	18. b	19. a	20. a
21. a	22. b	23. a	24. b	25. a	26. a	27. a	28. a	29. a	30. a
31. b	32. b	33. b	34. a	35. b	36. a	37. b	38. a	39. b	40. a
41. a	42. a	43. a	44. a	45. a	46. a	47. a	48. a	49. a	50. b
51. a	52. b	53. a	54. b	55. b	56. a	57. a	58. a	59. a	60. b
61. b	62. a	63. a	64. b	65. a	66. b	67. b	68. b	69. b	70. a
71. a	72. a	73. a	74. b	75. a	76. b	77. b	78. a	79. b	80. b
81. a	82. a	83. a	84. b	85. b	86. a	87. a			

Chapter 8

1. a	2. a	3. b	4. b	5. a	6. a	7. b	8. b	9. b	10. b
11. a	12. b	13. b	14. a	15. a	16. b	17. b	18. a	19. b	20. b
21. a	22. b	23. a	24. a	25. a	26. b	27. a	28. b	29. b	30. b
31. b	32. b	33. b	34. a	35. a	36. a	37. a	38. a	39. b	40. b
41. b	42. a	43. a	44. b	45. a	46. a	47. a	48. a	49. a	50. b
51. b	52. a	53. b	54. a	55. b	56. a	57. b	58. b	59. b	60. a
61. a	62. b	63. a	64. a	65. b	66. a	67. b			

Chapter 9

1. b	2. a	3. b	4. a	5. b	6. b	7. a	8. b	9. a	10. a
11. a	12. b	13. a	14. a	15. b	16. b	17. a	18. b	19. b	20. a
21. a	22. a	23. a	24. b	25. a	26. b	27. a	28. b	29. a	30. b
31. a	32. b	33. b	34. b	35. a	36. a	37. b	38. b	39. b	40. b
41. b	42. a	43. b	44. a	45. b	46. a	47. a	48. a	49. a	50. a
51. b	52. a	53. a	54. b	55. a	56. a	57. a	58. a	59. b	60. b
61. a	62. a	63. a	64. a	65. b	66. a	67. b	68. a	69. a	70. b
71. a	72. b	73. a	74. a	75. b	76. b	77. b	78. b	79. a	80. b
81. b	82. a	83. b	84. b	85. b	86. a	87. b	88. b	89. a	90. b
91. b	92. a	93. a	94. a	95. b	96. b	97. b	98. b	99. b	100. a
101. b	102. a	103. b	104. b	105. a	106. b				

Chapter 10

1. a	2. b	3. b	4. b	5. b	6. a	7. b	8. a	9. b	10. a
11. a	12. b	13. b	14. b	15. b	16. a	17. a	18. b	19. a	20. b
21. b	22. b	23. b	24. a	25. a	26. b	27. b	28. a	29. b	30. b
31. a	32. b	33. b	34. a	35. b	36. b	37. b	38. b	39. a	40. b
41. b	42. b	43. a	44. b	45. b	46. a	47. b	48. b	49. a	50. a
51. b	52. a	53. b	54. a